THE JESUS MIRACLE

Sophia R. Bailey

THE JESUS MIRACLE

Publisher Information

America Publishers
Email: info@americapublishers.com
Phone: +1 (617) 334-5774

ISBN Information

Paperback: 978-1-971854-04-5

Cover Design by: America Publishers

1st Edition: June, 2025

ABOUT THIS BOOK

This book originated from a vision I had received from the Lord approximately 30 years before the writing of the manuscript. (See my explanation of the vision in the Introduction chapter of the book.) I did not aspire to become an author, but after the vision, I had (unknowingly) made a promise to God that I would write the book one day.

As the dreams and visions increased and I noticed the pattern of spiritual and prophetic dreams, I started recording them all in a book, as I realised I did not know if God had a plan for me by giving me these dreams.

Let the reader note and understand that I am not a biblical scholar, I have no theological training, nor do I have any knowledge of Biblical languages or history (other than what is written in the Bible), nor do I claim to have a complete understanding or explanation of God's Word other than what was made known to me. What I am sharing with you is purely what the Holy Spirit has revealed to me over the years. Apart from the dreams and visions, I also received revelations through His word. I would, at times, receive a dream, and then at a later stage, the dream would be verified by a scripture verse, which astounded me. The Holy Spirit would also speak to me through the "still small voice" into my Spirit, and through scripture, thereby I could recognize when the Lord had spoken to me, for He says, "My sheep hear my voice."

In this book, I reference several scriptures, as all the revelations I received relate to scriptures. Thus, the reader can be assured of the truth of my testimony and His Word.

Revelation 12 verse 11: "And they overcame him by the blood of the Lamb, and by the Word of their testimony; and they did not love their lives to the death."

I consider myself blessed, being chosen by God to reveal Himself to me through His Spirit, through dreams and visions and His word. At one stage of my life, I became hungry for His word and eager to learn from it and to know God and have a personal relationship with the Lord Jesus. I am just sharing what God has revealed to me in ways that I can comprehend. I believe that He saw my heart and prepared me to be obedient to His instructions and to share what He has taught me with others who are searching for meaning and truth.

The Gospel is not difficult to understand. The apostle Paul says that *"we need not that anyone should teach us"* if the Holy Spirit is our teacher. He also says, *"The wisdom of this world is foolishness to God, for it is written that He catches the wise in their craftiness." And again, the Lord knows the thoughts of the wise, that they are futile." (1 Corinthians 3 verses 19-20).* (NKJV) Therefore, I do not claim to be wise according to the standards of the world; on the contrary, I profess to have only the Holy Spirit to credit my knowledge of scripture and my understanding of who Jesus is. Also, I have God's word hidden in my heart so I can at all times call upon His Word.

I will not be able to debate wise scholars based on acquired knowledge through the study of scripture and ancient texts because I think that I am wise, but only through the wisdom of the Holy Spirit am I able to make my case, for He will speak for me."

We must humble ourselves before God, no matter how smart we are. Pause for a moment and think about how the Eternal God has humbled Himself to become like us. There can be no humiliation lower than that - it is incomprehensible. It should not be that difficult for a man to humble himself under the Mighty Hand of God. Humility is what God requires of us to reveal Himself to us, and scripture promises that "He will exalt us in due time."

We think we know everything, but we know so little. We do not know what we do not know, especially spiritual things, because we can't see into the spiritual realm. But with the Spirit of God dwelling inside of us, He reveals spiritual things to us in ways we can understand. I always compare our lack of knowledge and understanding due to our physical nature and limitation to the earthly realm to, for example, a fish living in the ocean. It knows nothing apart from the environment it lives in. A fish has no idea of the wide, wide world where humans dwell. How can he know? Therefore, we do not know the things of the Spirit, for "they are spiritually discerned."

Another scripture I want to refer to is found in 1 Corinthians 1, verses 27 to 28, in which the Apostle Paul talks about how the things that we humans consider wise are foolishness to God. *"For He has chosen the foolish things of the world to put to shame the wise and chosen the weak things of the world to put to shame the things that are mighty and the base things of the world and the things which are despised, God has chosen."* (NKJV)

Having stated this, it is no offense to the wise but only relates to the things of God revealed by His Spirit because the things of God are "spiritually discerned."

We cannot understand spiritual things with our natural minds.

Jeremiah 9 verse 23: "Let not the wise man glory in His wisdom. Let not the mighty man glory in his might. Nor let the rich man glory in his riches. But let him who glories, glory in this that he understands and knows Me that I Am the Lord, exercising loving-kindness, judgment, and righteousness in the earth. For in these I delight, says the Lord." (NKJV)

God does not do things in ways that we can understand. That is why we sometimes cannot comprehend His way of doing things in our lives."

Isaiah 55 verse 9: "For as the heavens are higher than the earth, so are My ways higher than your ways and My thoughts than your thoughts." (NKJV)

This book was written under the inspiration, instruction, guidance, and will of the Holy Spirit, who called me to fulfill the task He had chosen for me. He has revealed Himself to me by His Spirit, and I can truly say that the Holy Spirit was my teacher in learning the word of God. It is not of my own fleshly desire but an "assignment" from Him. If any of the teachings I had received were contrary to the Word of God, I would have rejected them. But since the revelations align with scripture, I was convicted by the truth of it.

"Not by might nor by power but by My Spirit, "says the Lord." Zechariah 4 verse 6. (NKJV)

It is out of obedience to God, to give Him glory, to do my part in bringing the Gospel to those who are seeking, to share my experiences in which the Holy Spirit has made known to me the ways in which He communicates with us. I became very hungry for the Word, though I did not understand it fully.

Because of my hunger for the Word and also because I had asked Him for insight and more revelation to understand more of scripture, He willingly imparted this gift to me. In one of my dreams, the Hand of God poured water onto me from a cloud, which I later discovered in scripture attests to the meaning that God would make His words known to me.

Every person may not experience hearing from the Lord the same way that I did, but each one will hear from God in their own unique way, as He has bestowed different spiritual gifts upon His children for those who are seeking Him and are hungry for His Word.

Jeremiah 23 verse 28: "The prophet who has a dream let him tell a dream. And he who has My word let him speak My Word faithfully" (NKJV)

CONTENTS

INTRODUCTION

In this introduction, I am referencing a number of scriptures relating to my dreams and visions from the Lord.

While reading this book, please keep in mind the following two scripture verses as they directly relate to my dreams and visions.

Job 33 verse 14-16: "For God may speak in one way or another, yet man does not perceive it. In a dream or in a vision of the night. When deep sleep falls upon man, when slumbering on their beds, then He opens the ears of man and seals their instructions." (NKJV)

Numbers 12 verse 6: "If there is a prophet among you, I the Lord make myself known to him in a vision, I speak to him in a dream."(NKJV)

This book is the product of a vision that I had received from the Lord approximately 30 years prior to the writing of the manuscript. Here is the vision:

I had been slumbering on my bed when a vision of a book appeared before my eyes in the Spirit. The cover of the book that I saw was red, and the book was titled *"The Jesus Miracle."* At the bottom of the cover, there was a depiction of the two grey stone tablets with the Ten Commandments engraved on them in an ancient language that I did not understand. I woke up from this vision and sensed in my Spirit, saying, "I will write this book someday." What I did not realise was that I had made a promise to God by affirming that I would write the book. Years had passed, and the book never came to fruition. At times, I had forgotten about it, but God did not forget.

Throughout the years, I did not know what God wanted the content of the book to be. I certainly did not know what the theme of the book would be. I reasoned by myself. Whether the theme of the book should be about the works that Jesus had performed throughout His ministry on earth or whether it should be about the Miracle of God Himself becoming a man. I tend to lean more towards the doctrine of God in human form than the miracles He had performed, although the miracles He had performed while on the earth should not be curtailed. Therefore, I waited for His instructions.

The years went by, and I would, at times, just forget about the "assignment." However, as time passed, God, in His divine wisdom, continued giving me dreams and visions, continually speaking to me through His Word and through the "still small voice" of the Holy Spirit. God had also given me the ability to interpret some of my dreams through revelation from the Holy Spirit, but other dreams were not revealed to me yet.

What was unbeknown to me was that God was indeed preparing me for the authoring of "His" book as He opened my understanding to His Word and revealed knowledge to me through dreams. At the time, I was puzzled as to why I was receiving all the spiritual and prophetic dreams and information, but after many years, I began to understand why I had to go through the "training processes" in my life. Things started falling into place, coming together like a jigsaw puzzle. God had a plan all along, and He worked through it systematically in His wisdom and, at the same time, had to do a work in me, drawing me closer to Him and enabling me to discern His Voice. It took a very long time for me to clearly understand when He spoke.

I do not proclaim myself a prophet, but in the sense that the Lord had spoken to me in dreams and visions, I will let the truth of my experiences speak for itself. (I prefer to remain His humble maidservant). God has blessed each of His children with spiritual gifts, and He has blessed me with this gift of prophetic and spiritual dreams and the revelation of the person and divinity of Jesus Christ. Not only did the Lord bless and speak to me in dreams and visions, but He also made His Words "known to me."

God has given me the wisdom and revelation of the knowledge of Him (Christ Jesus) of His own will, for which I am forever grateful.

Sometimes, the message was for the body of Christ, and sometimes, it was meant for me personally, for my own spiritual growth, knowledge, and understanding of Him. I have found the grace in this time to fulfil my promise to Him after realising what the message should be that He wanted me to bring to His people. In His perfect time, God made everything come together, and the vision became clear.

The vision that the prophet Habakkuk wrote about reminds me of the vision that I received from the Lord so many years ago, which I did not understand when it was imparted to me.

Habakkuk 2 verse 3: "For the vision is yet for an appointed time, but at the end of it it will speak and will not lie. Though it tarries, wait for it because it will surely come. It will not tarry." (NKJV)

A fire was rekindled in me towards the end of 2024 to start writing the book, and once I dived into it, the words just started flowing from my heart, through the pen, onto the pages. He made known to me the meaning of some of my dreams through scripture that I had not understood before. I enjoyed writing this book once I decided it was time to proceed. I took delight in the renewed knowledge and understanding of what my task is and how to bring it to fulfilment. In a dream, God had a golden pen delivered to me from heaven into my right hand, so I believed it to be a mandate from Him, which is why everything came together so easily in the end. The "J.C." pen served its purpose, and I could proceed with joy and certainty of the knowledge that the Holy Spirit was working through me, His vessel, and the pen in His Hand, with the daunting task of writing down every word that I perceived the Holy Spirit was guiding me by. See my dream about the golden pen from heaven in Chapter 8, c.

As the dreams and visions became more frequent with time, I realised that there must be a reason why I was getting them. There seemed to be a sequence of spiritual revelations to it, but I did not understand it at that time. I started taking notes, and I decided to start keeping a record of them in a diary.

Although God had given me dreams and spiritual knowledge, this book is primarily about the revelation of Jesus (Yeshua). God has shown me that Jesus is the "High and Mighty One enthroned on the praises of His people."

I haven't been faithful in the beginning since I haven't committed to His plans for my life - plans that God had intended for me. Also, I did not take it too seriously, as, at the time, I did not plan to make Him the centre of my life. I knew that there was a calling from God upon my life, but I did not know what to do about it and how to go about it. During this time of doubting and delaying, I had a dream wherein God reprimanded me for, I guess, not taking Him seriously about His calling, in which He said to me, *"I spoke, and you did not listen. I spoke again, and you did not understand."* I was so slow in learning the things of the Spirit. It took me years to understand that God had an assignment for me for His plans and His purposes, and I just couldn't get it. (Jeremiah 7 verse 13 *says: "And I spoke to you, rising up early and speaking, but you did not hear and calling you, but you did not answer." (NKJV) (I had been hard of hearing the call of the Spirit for so many years.*

The cares of life sidetracked me, and I lost vision and hope that I could ever serve the purpose of my calling. It became my heart's desire to serve the Lord in a full-time capacity. However, I never lost that dream, the promise to God that I would write a book about the things that He had taught me, especially the Revelation of Christ Jesus, to me personally. Having said this, I always believed that Jesus is the God of creation. I needed no proof from Him to reveal Himself to me (because I believed it in my heart.) I didn't ask Him to prove to me who Jesus is, yet it was His will to give me these revelations to strengthen my faith and to share these revelations with the body of Christ.

God had remained faithful to me, even though I had almost given up at times. In my natural mind, I could not fathom how the Lord could put all of the broken pieces of my shattered life together after more than 30 years of procrastination.

Jesus never gives up on us, no matter how unfaithful we become, because scripture says that "He cannot be unfaithful to Himself," as we are all part of Him.

At the time of writing this book, I had lost much of my vision (eyesight) and my health. I realised that I did not have a choice but to complete my task, for when I was young and healthy, I did not have the courage and the "knowing" to embark on the journey, which I totally regret now.

I have been through many trials, especially the last number of years, suffering in every aspect of my life and sometimes almost lost hope that He would come through for me. The worst part of my suffering was my health, and it got so bad at times that I thought I could not go on living with the pain anymore. But many people prayed and interceded for me, and God has been faithful because there was a definite change in my health, although not everything in my life had improved. I did not die as I wanted to, for my assignment had not been completed yet.

I mention this to make a point that when there is a call on one's life from God, then you'd better be ready for sacrifice and hardship. In fact, there was a time when the Holy Spirit spoke a word into "my heart repeatedly, and He said, build an altar, build an altar." These words were going through my mind over and over, but I did not know what He had meant. Nothing is going smoothly when you are walking the way of the cross. The enemy will attack you at all times because he wants you to quit, but you have to keep going in your walk with Christ.

We have to take up our cross and follow Him. Believers are called righteous because Christ is our righteousness. *"We are saved by grace and not of*

ourselves; it is a gift of God so that no one could boast."
Ephesians 2 verse 8 (NKJV)

My dreams and visions are not extra-biblical revelations, but it is aligned with scripture. I am certainly not bringing "another gospel" to you. I trust that nobody will feel that my message is not in line with scripture, but instead, I urge you to search the scriptures for yourselves to test my message to see whether it is true. Anyone can learn something valuable from this book because it can aid others in their spiritual walk with God. But please bear in mind that Scripture should be our first and main source in learning God's Word. I do advise you to also pray about my message in this book and, as always, ask the Holy Spirit to reveal the truth to you. My heart has been exceedingly sad for many years for my brethren who have been led astray by strange doctrines.

Jesus Christ is the wisdom of God, and only through the revelation of Him can we say that He is Lord. *"For the testimony of Jesus is the Spirit of prophecy. Revelation 19, verse 10. (NKJV)*

In Chapter 2g, I talk about the encounter that I had with an angel of light. My understanding is that people who receive messages from "Angels" to take to others are probably being deceived, especially if they do not know the Word and do not have spiritual discernment to see whether it is of God. The Bible says that even Satan himself can appear as an angel of light.

In Jesus Christ was the full and final revelation of God's Word. Any new message that came after the manifestation of Christ is not of God. God had said what He wanted to say to humanity through Jesus Christ because Christ was the fulfilment of the Law. Jesus said, "I did not come to abolish the Law but to fulfil it." We should always ask God for spiritual wisdom and discernment about new teachings, for without discernment, many people are being led astray by deceiving spirits and "doctrines of demons." God has placed a burden in my heart, not only for the lost but also for people who are led astray so easily by the teachings of man simply because they do not know the Word. Bear in mind, we need no other teaching from anyone, even if it is from an Angel - we do have God's Word, and we only need to heed His Word, believe that His Word is true, and be obedient to His commandments."

Helping people to understand the simplicity, beauty, and truth of scripture, the knowledge, and the understanding of the Holy One of Israel will be a great honour, blessing, and privilege for me. I want people to "taste and see that the Lord is good." Having said that, it doesn't mean that we will not encounter suffering and hardship. Every believer will have to endure some time or other, and to some extent, what it is to follow Christ. But we need to be encouraged to look to the upward call of God, to run the race with endurance, to finish strong, and at last receive our crowns in Glory.

My mission is to bring God glory, to help people know and understand who Jesus (Yeshua) is, to encourage people to study and know the word of God and to become anchored in the truth of God's word.

It is also my desire to give birth to my destiny of authoring this book for His glory, by His Word, and by the leading of His Holy Spirit.

I hope that this book will be of great insight and blessing to all who read it, and I pray that the Lord will fill you with His wisdom, knowledge, discernment, understanding, and the knowledge of Christ Jesus. Having said this, it doesn't mean that you do not need to rely on scripture. On the contrary, scripture is still God's authoritative message to humanity, and so I encourage everyone to read and study the Word daily.

Lastly, by sharing my experiences of His revelations to me through my dreams, I hope that this book might be an evangelising tool for the advancement of the Gospel and for people to give praise and glory to Jesus, the King of Kings.

Chapter 1:
Humble Beginnings

Since a very young age, I have always had the sense that God had chosen me for a purpose. I had no idea what it could be and why I felt that way since my knowledge of scripture and of the spiritual reality was almost non-existent. Looking back, I now understand that the Holy Spirit had always been present in my life, speaking and guiding me without me knowing it. I was raised in the Catholic faith, so I always knew that Jesus was real, that He was born on Christmas day (or so we were told), and that He was crucified for our sins. However, I did not understand the spiritual implications of the enormity of what God had done for the world through the crucified Christ. We used to sing Christmas songs and many other Christian Hymns, yet we did not understand in our hearts that we were worshipping the true God – the God of Israel.

I learned the rituals and traditions of the church, but I did not learn much of scripture – we did not read the Bible as young people, so we only knew what we were taught about church doctrines and what we had heard from others, as well as being influenced by our culture.

I was raised in an impoverished family of 11 children, Seven (7) sons and four (4) daughters, of which I was the 8th in the family. God has blessed me with spiritual and prophetic dreams and visions, but at the time (in my youth), I had no awareness or understanding that God had bestowed upon me a spiritual gift that I didn't ask for or even dreamed about, neither did I understand anything of this calling on my life then. I cannot say for certain when exactly I learned about Jesus. I came into the world always knowing about Him. As you will see later from a Word God has given me, I wondered if I had known about Him in my mother's womb already because scripture says that we are "fearfully and wonderfully made." In His wisdom and power, I believe that God can communicate with babies in the womb. Therefore, we could not possibly understand His heart for the harm caused to the innocents in the mother's womb.

As a person, I was a real "introvert" in my school days. I never had fights with anybody, but I was bullied at primary school, yet I did not tell anyone about it. I never wanted to draw attention to myself – I would always remain in the background, not wanting to be noted. Humiliation and degradation were part of my childhood, especially by school teachers who did not fully understand the implications of preparing children to become healthy, good adults for life ahead.

Most of my revelations were dreams. Therefore, if I do not mention it to be a vision, then just know it is a dream. The exception is the encounters I had in Chapter 2, which were real encounters that I found strange and, therefore, had no explanation for those specific incidents. There is another inexplicable encounter with my bible in Chapter 8 about my calling in which the Lord tried to get my attention with His Word.

Growing up in the sixties, I had no vision for my future, as sad as that may sound, but God did have a plan for me that He wanted me to strive for, entering through the narrow gate by teaching me the power and truth of knowing His Word. I did not desire to live in wealth and luxury or even to have my own home. I just live because God has put me on the earth. I had no ambition other than becoming a pianist, but my parents could not afford to send any of their children for any educational training.

My siblings and I had been through many, many days of hunger, but it never dawned on us to blame our parents for being hungry because they had suffered with us. We lived through apartheid and knew firsthand how every negative policy had affected our lives, but even through all that, we never had any hatred toward white people. We did not understand that being judged according to the colour of one's skin was morally wrong. We were children, and we thought that it was just the way life was. We just lived and enjoyed our childhood - we did not worry about the problems that the adults had to deal with.

Because my father was not liked in the town, his children were all ridiculed, ostracised, and belittled by people who rejected him as if he did not belong. He was not the "bad guy" in town, but he was not liked, and sadly, his children also had to pay for that. Out of respect for the memory of my late father, I will not go into details, as we all loved and respected him as our dad.

CHAPTER 2
STRANGE ENCOUNTERS

A) CHILDLIKE PRAYER

"A family that prays together stays together," so the saying goes. We never prayed together as a family, but as a little girl, I knew how to pray. Nobody taught me how to pray, but I approached God in childlike faith, and I know that God appreciated and loved the innocence and obedience of a child. I remember once I went down on my knees to pray for my family, especially my father and mother. When I got off my knees, I got the smell of sweet perfume. There was nobody with me, so I did not know what to make of it. In hindsight, I thought that maybe my childlike prayer was acceptable to Him.

B) FLOATING ON CLOUDS

As a little girl, I regularly experienced the sensation that I was drifting away on soft, fluffy white clouds. It happened every time I would close my eyes to go to sleep. It was a strange but exhilarating sensation. I was enveloped by a soft tenderness, an awareness that there was something, a presence greater than what I could perceive. I also felt like I was drifting through space like a light white feather. These encounters stopped as I became older, but I always kept it in my heart. I realised by this experience that there is a spirit within man and that we are not flesh and blood only.

C) Unknown longing

In my teenage years, I used to go through times with an unknown longing inside my soul to be somewhere else, away from this world. I had a real sense that there was more to this world than what we could perceive with our natural minds. I am sure many people have experienced this before. I did not really understand then the concept of who God is, but when I came to the knowledge of Him, I understood that that was the empty void in my human heart reserved for the Creator only. When I reminisced about this, then I would also receive a word in my Spirit (which was actually in scripture in the bible) about "*those who love their lives will lose it, and he who hates his life in this world will keep it*" This is a scripture found in John 12 verse 25. I did not understand where that came from as I did not yet read the Bible at that stage, nor did I know anything in scripture, but it touched me deeply. The sense that I did not belong here on earth was so overwhelming, and it made me sad that I did not understand the longing inside. I know today that the Holy Spirit has been working in my life for as long as I can remember for His glory and His purposes.

D) Visiting Angel

It was a bright moonlight night when the dogs started barking at the sound of little bells at the approaching of a tall, dark stranger. I imagined that the stranger had bells tied around his ankles (although I did not see them) that sounded with every step he took. We were six families living on a little hill just outside town – all houses just consisted of one room. Our house was number 5, and the stranger approached our house directly.

I was very young (about 7-8 years old), Intrigued by this person and what he was doing there. I watched and listened intently as he approached my mother for a place to sleep, although I cannot remember in what language he communicated with my mother, in their body language, I could see that there had been a conversation between them.

I was captivated by that tall, dark stranger wearing a bright white jumpsuit which was in stark contrast to his very dark skin. We had no food in the house but I remember my mother giving him a piece of dry bread and water. There was a single iron cast bed outside on the veranda and mom did her best to make it comfortable for him to sleep in. I do not even remember if there was a mattress for the bed, nevertheless, he seemed to be fine with it. I knew in my heart that my mother did the right thing by entertaining the stranger because that is who she was – a kind and humble woman owning nothing but just living and sacrificing for her children. In my heart, I was pleased that she gave the man a place to rest.

When I woke up the next morning, my first thought was to check out the stranger properly in the daylight, but to my disappointment, he was gone and I was very sad to not get to see his face since I was so intrigued by him. The incident left an enduring imprint on my soul and later on, I couldn't help but wonder if he was an angel, as I had always thought about it. I never questioned my mother about it, neither did I ask any of my siblings if they had witnessed the visiting stranger. Hebrews 13:2 *"Do not forget to entertain strangers, for by doing so, some have unwittingly entertained angels."* *(NKJV)*

I did not know about this word, about entertaining strangers at the time, but I knew that my mom had done what was right. Years later, when I became more knowledgeable in scripture and read this text, I couldn't help but wonder if, indeed, an angel had visited us.

E) Intuitive warnings

I. Snake warning

There was a certain tree in the fields where I used to go and lie under its shade to study during the hot summer days. On one particular day, I fell asleep and had a dream of a snake. The snake came to lie right there by my head, and in the dream, I had a warning to lie very still and not to move. How long it went on, I did not know, but the whole time I had to be still, my heart was pounding, and I was panicking. Eventually, when I woke up, I knew that there was a real snake in the vicinity because I could sense the danger. I jumped up, my adrenaline pumping, grabbed my books and ran home. Needless to say, I never returned there again!

II. Snake alert

In another encounter with a snake, my siblings and I went for a drive into the wilderness on a dusty road. My sister wanted to drive the car, so I stopped and got out of the car to enable her to drive. I told them to go ahead and that I would follow them on foot as I needed the exercise. I just walked a few steps when I suddenly received a warning in my Spirit about a snake. I froze in my tracks and couldn't wait for them to return. I was scared. I did not move forward or backward. When they eventually came back, my brother told me that they saw a snake lying in the middle of the road. I was astounded by the warning I had received in my Spirit.

I learned from this experience that we do need to take heed of warnings in our Spirit. That is just another way by which God protects us, no matter where we are. We need our spiritual eyes and ears to be open to the voice of the Holy Spirit. Therefore, a warning from God can be about anything at any time. We just need to pay attention to the "small still voice" within us.

F) Picture in the clouds

On a very hot summer's day, as I was watching the clouds forming interesting shapes and patterns, I noticed different shapes that the clouds had formed, but the shape that intrigued me the most was the shape of a king sitting on his throne with a crown on his head. I thought that it was very interesting and that the king sitting on his throne may be representative of the King of heaven. That cloud shape, for some reason, never left my mind - it always stayed with me until now. I mention these little incidents because they were adding to my insight into the reality of the way in which little things not worthy of paying attention to, are happening all around us, things we just dismiss as insignificant. I see these small incidents as enriching to my Spirit and in the understanding of the way in which God communicates with us.

G) ANGEL OF LIGHT

This encounter came about one night in 1982, as I was asleep on my bed when some very bright flickering lights came shining through the window into my room, going round and round in circles on the walls. It was a bewildering encounter. I had never experienced anything like it. This was a spiritual encounter, and I did not know how to deal with it - it was not anything that I could reason out in my natural mind. I found myself out of my body (I assume from the shock of seeing a Spirit before my eyes), my Spirit up on the ceiling watching the scene outside the window through my spiritual eyes. (The curtains were drawn closed, yet I was able to see through it with my spirit eyes.) I received some communication from this entity of light that He was God and that I needed to get up from the bed and come and face him at the window. I noticed that He did not say that he was Jesus, so my Spirit did not recognise him. God cannot appear to humans as God, because we will die - we cannot see God. He is far beyond our understanding. I think also that this is why many people do not believe in Him, because they cannot see Him. But I do think that He can appear as the "Angel of the Lord", which happened many times in the Old Testament to the prophets.

I sensed fear and panic, and I was not able to get up from my bed and go to the window. It was an angel of light, and it was emanating light – the light that went around in circles in my room. The way I can describe the angel is that it appeared to look like the visions of the "Virgin Mary" as portrayed by the Catholic Church, except that light emanated from it.

I shared this encounter with one of my sisters, but she was very disappointed that I did not obey the angel because she thought that the angel might have had an important message for me. The Bible warns us that even Satan can appear to us as an angel of light and also that we must test the spirits. In this case, it did not mention the Name of Jesus, and my Spirit did not recognise that Spirit.

May I remind the reader of what Paul says in Galatians 1 verse 8: "But even if we or an Angel from heaven preach any other gospel to you than what we have received, let him be accursed. Further on, in verse 10, Paul says, "For I neither received it nor was I taught it, but it came through the revelation of Jesus Christ." (NKJV)

H) TONGUE OF FIRE

This incident happened to me also in the early eighties. I was on my bed dozing off, but I wasn't asleep, although my eyes were closed. I noticed a blue/white tongue of fire hovering above my head, and it shocked me as I did not know what it was. The natural reaction was to open my eyes to see it better, but it was not there. I then realised that I had seen it with my spirit eyes and I was reminded of the tongues of fire that came upon the apostles at the time of Pentecost. (Acts 2 verse 3

I) JOHN THE BAPTIST "FIGURE"

On a certain day, I went to the central part of the city with my friends, where we were going to take part in a sports event called "The Twilight Run". We were standing on the sidewalk, waiting for the first group of athletes to pass. In the group that came into focus, I noticed a strange-looking person dressed very strangely and immediately the name "John the Baptist" came into my mind. He was tall with light brown curly hair, a bronze brownish skin colour, and he was wearing brown leather and animal skin clothing. He looked strange and did not seem to fit into the crowd. He seemed like a homeless man, but at the same time, like someone very significant. His tall stature made him appear very confident and very important. The moment I fixed my eyes on him, he looked back at me with a telling expression on his face. I saw His lips moving, and he lifted his eyes towards heaven as if praying, his lips moving. He would then look back at me with a friendly expression on his face. He would do that a couple of times, making gestures and movements with his arms. He later disappeared into the crowd.

I was captured by the presence of that stranger, and in my own mind, I believed him to be a messenger angel among us.

J) WATCHER ANGELS

I was at a special church meeting where a highly respected pastor from the US came to speak. I took my seat as the building was still filling up slowly, and I was very excited for the meeting to start. As time progressed, I heard someone laughing. It did not bother me at that moment. However, another person started laughing, then another and another, and it started to increase, so much so that I started giggling as well because of how funny the laughter sounded. As the laughter increased, I started getting worried because it began to sound like demonic laughter. I noticed two people standing at the back of me, two rows behind me to my right. They seemed strange as if they were worried about something. They kept looking at me, and I did the same in return by looking back at them. I began to sense something creepy and unholy in that place. I questioned God in my heart about that, and in the meantime, I kept looking back at the strange couple. In my Spirit, I got the impression that they were angels sent to watch over me. Eventually, I decided to leave the meeting, but just before I decided to go, they had also left, and I knew it was time for me to go.

On my way home, I questioned God about the things I had witnessed that night, telling Him that I did not believe that "phenomena" was from Him. My answer came from Him the same night when I opened my bible and was given 1 Timothy 4 verse 1: *"Now the Spirit expressly says that in latter times some will depart from the faith, giving heed to deceiving spirits and doctrines of demons." (NKJV)*

I was satisfied that God had answered me to put my Spirit to rest.

K) A BUTTERFLY COMPANION

On the farm where I received training as a missionary, I was left alone one week – everybody had left for a break. I was working on the computer in our Evangelism Team leader's apartment. At about 10 o'clock, I decided to call it a day and shut down the computer to go to my apartment for a good night's rest. As I opened the door to leave the house, a butterfly flew out the door ahead of me. I did not know that there was a butterfly in the house with me. It was beautiful, brown and orange with black and white spots on its wings.

My flat was about 100 steps away from the house on the opposite side, so I still had to turn left and go up three steps to get to my door. It was dark outside, and I had lost sight of my winged companion.

As I opened my front door, and out of nowhere, the winged creature flew into the apartment first before I could put my foot into the place. I then tried to get it out of the flat without hurting it, but it wouldn't go, so I left it alone and went to my room to get ready for a bath while my "watcher friend" was just sitting there on the wall in the passage.

As I went into the bathroom, the butterfly once again flew in first before I got to the bathroom. I decided to leave him alone, so he just sat there on the wall of the bathroom, probably watching that I'd be ok. I came out of the bathroom, and he came flying out after me (note: after) and it went to sit on the wall again in the passage opposite my bedroom door for the whole night. The next morning (I had forgotten about it), when I opened the door, he flew out the door. I thought that was so cool that God had sent an angel to watch over me.

All the above encounters happened, and I found them strange and inexplicable, but they also gave me the assurance that God is present in our daily lives and He allows us to witness things to make us aware that there is a spiritual reality.

CHAPTER 3
AN OPEN VISION

GOD REVEALING HIS LOVE

It happened suddenly and unexpectedly one day at work while I was busy typing a document. The vision I had left me shaken, puzzled and bewildered. While going about my task, I suddenly and without warning received a very powerful open vision of many people milling around in a big city, each one going about their own business. A question came into my mind from the Holy Spirit asking, "Do you see all these people?" In my Spirit, I answered yes. Then an answer came back to me saying: "THEY ARE ALL LOST APART FROM ME." (I then knew that it was Jesus speaking to me in my Spirit)

At the same time these words were communicated to me, my Spirit was flooded with God's Love, mercy and compassion for humanity. It was an overwhelming, unknown emotional encounter as if cold water was being poured onto me. It caused great turmoil within me, it moved me to tears and left me bewildered and in shock. I ran out of the office to a secluded room where I could process the vision that I had just encountered. The tears were running down my face, and I did not want my colleagues to see me crying as my thoughts were that I would not be able to explain to anyone what I had just encountered. I did not understand it myself. I remember thinking, "Where did that come from?" I could never have felt such immense love and compassion for mankind within myself. But then the Holy Spirit made it known to me that God has given me just a taste of His love and mercy for humanity – scripture says that *"God is not willing that anyone should perish but that all should come to Him in repentance and live." 2 Peter 3 verse 9. (NKJV)*

As God had given me a revelation of His love for humanity, so has he allowed my Spirit to encounter spiritual darkness for reasons known only to Himself.

I was never the same after this encounter with the living Jesus. In the days and weeks that followed, I was burdened with a very heavy burden for the lost. I went through this time of spiritual darkness, not knowing what to do about it. I could not sleep, I had lost my appetite, and there was an enormous change that took place in my spiritual being. The weight was so heavy for me to carry that I even lost my will to live. The way I can describe it is that my soul was weeping for the lost. I was aware that my Spirit within me was weeping for people. It was like a bitter lament, but there were no physical tears. My Spirit was weeping, and there was no way I could stop it. My prayers for the lost became more earnest and more intercessory, but I received no comfort. I lost interest in everything around me. It was hard for me to get up and go to work every day. Looking around me and seeing people going about their lives, blissfully unaware of the danger their souls were facing", I would cringe in fear for them. My Spirit was weeping for them. I felt like the scripture says in *Jeremiah 13 verse 17, "My soul wept in secret for your pride. My eyes will weep bitterly and run down with tears."* (NKJV) I went through a very traumatic time and couldn't go on with my life, so I prayed that God would take away the burden from me, as it was too heavy for me to bear. *Psalm 119 verse 29" My soul melts from heaviness. Strengthen me according to Your Word." (NKJV)*

Gradually, the burden started lifting from my soul, and I started feeling "normal" again. Years later, I regretted asking God to lift the burden off of me because I did not know what He had intended to accomplish through this encounter with me as His vessel. It may be that I was not spiritually mature enough to go through with His special assignment He had for me. (Lord, I publicly ask for your forgiveness for my disobedience.) I felt like Jonah trying to run away from his calling. But he never gave up on me. (Blessed be His Holy Name).

The vision that I had left me a completely changed person. The transformation I had been going through was permanent. I lost all desire for the things of the world, and my burden for the lost has remained. I woke up from a dream one night, sobbing with a deep sorrow in my Spirit for those who do not know Jesus.

I continued on my walk with God, praying for the lost and developed the desire to become a full-time missionary.

CHAPTER 4
IN PURSUIT OF GOD

A) MY FIRST BIBLE

On the 10th of March 1980, I was given the priceless gift of my own Bible by a Catholic priest. It was the "Good News" translation which I started reading immediately. I did not understand much of the spiritual aspects of the Old Testament, but I did understand some of the history in the Bible. The New Testament opened my eyes to the person and divinity of Christ, and the words that I read became embedded in my heart. Words that I had never heard before. I found a great treasure in the Word of God. Psalm 119 verse 162 says, "*I rejoice at Your Word as one who has found a great treasure.*"

Psalm 51 quickly became my favourite passage in scripture, and for some reason, I had learned to recite it, and it spoke right into my heart. Psalm 51 is about a repentant heart and the mercies of God. This Psalm became a regular prayer for me throughout my life.

Psalm 91 also became one of my favourite Psalms, and I learned to memorise this as well. As I continued to study scripture, God would reveal more and more of His words to me. Sometimes, I would read a word, and I would receive a revelation about it, while, as I read the same word before, I did not discern the truth of the scripture or a light that would enlighten my mind.

The book of Isaiah became an absolute treasure regarding the prophecy of the promised Messiah. The truth written in it became like refreshing living water for my soul because Jesus was the fulfilment of all those prophecies.

B) Learning from Scripture

I was delighted to discover all the hidden treasures in scripture, and I was so impacted by it that I started doing my own "private" Bible study. I learned about the person of Jesus, how He was prophesied about in the Old Testament and how He became the only person in history to fulfil all those prophecies. God had revealed it to me Himself, and until today, I am at a loss for words as to how people cannot believe that Jesus is Lord. I once argued with a Muslim guy about the divinity of Jesus, and he assured me that he had also read the Bible but that he didn't agree with me. You may read the Bible a million times, but if the Holy Spirit does not open your eyes to your spiritual understanding, then you will not know and understand in your heart who Jesus is. You will have to ask Him to reveal Himself to you. After all, the Bible is the Living Word of God.

C) THE HOLY SPIRIT IS MY TEACHER

The Holy Spirit had become my guide and teacher throughout the learning and searching process of His truth. The Word became alive to my Spirit, and the truth of scripture became evident and undeniable. I am truly blessed that He was my teacher throughout my learning of the Scriptures. Also, God has blessed me with discernment whereby I will not be misled by every wind of doctrine, as He is always there to guide and protect me. "He is my Rock and my Salvation."

"Forever, O Lord, Your Word is settled in heaven." *Psalm 119 verse 89. (NKJV)*

No one speaking by the Spirit of God calls Jesus accursed, and no one can say that Jesus is Lord except by the Holy Spirit" 1 Corinthians 12 verse 3. (NKJV)

As is evident through the dreams, visions and scripture that the Lord had imparted to me, the wisdom to know and understand His Word. The Spirit played a pivotal role in my training as a seeker of truth and a seeker of the Living Lord.

D) HUNGRY FOR THE WORD

The more I read the Word, the hungrier and thirstier I became for more of the bread of life and the living waters. As I continued to devour scripture and my Spirit was fed, my faith grew stronger, and I no longer lived on milk only but on solid food of the Word. I remember thinking when I was younger that I had never grown tired of hearing the story of Jesus, no matter how many sermons I listened to or how many movies or videos I had watched over the years. This story of the God of all creation, willing to prepare a body for Himself, becoming like one of us and giving Himself as an offering for sin just to reconcile us to Himself, is mind-boggling. The greatness of His love for humanity is incomprehensible. It's beyond our understanding. All the Lord wants from us is to love Him with all our hearts, to love our brother like ourselves, to be obedient to His Word and to fear Him. Also, I reasoned by myself that God has given us His commandments for our good. If we transgress His commandments, then we will have to take upon ourselves the consequences of our deeds. If we confess our sins, He is ready to forgive, however, we will still suffer the consequences of our deeds, whether good or evil. Whatever it is that we sow, we will reap.

My soul had embarked on a pious journey to find out more about the One I was hungry for – to experience more of Him. It was during this stage of my life that I developed the desire to go on missions. I wanted to "change" the world for Christ.

In the meantime, God had spoken to me through more and more dreams, prophetic and spiritual, and it enriched my Spirit a great deal.

E) MY QUEST FOR JESUS

I wanted to know more about the person of Jesus, and the more I read about Him in the scriptures, the more I believed Him to be God in the flesh. He is such a remarkable person, and to me, there was such power and authority in His words and actions, healing the sick, cleansing the lepers, raising the dead, and Him claiming to be God in the flesh by saying (amongst other claims) "Before Abraham was born, I AM". He had the power to forgive sin, and the people questioned as to who could forgive sin but God.

In Chapter 5, I detailed my dreams in which Jesus revealed Himself to me in many different ways.

F) His Name is power - The Name of Jesus

I became so spirit-driven that I had a dream one night that I was flying through space to find God. I was travelling through the starry night skies, observing all the trillions of stars in the heavens. I heard myself saying, "Where are You, Lord?" I love and adore you so much, I will do anything for you." After saying these words, I heard demonic laughter all around me as if they were mocking me for my pitiful and weak attempt to find God. I then started rebuking the demons in the Name of Jesus. I heard my voice echoing through space. The demonic laughter stopped, they had gone dead silent, and I could sense their fear at the mention of the Name of Jesus. The dream ended before I could find Him!!

In a separate dream, I experienced being sucked out of my head, going through space. I objected and fought against it. It happened a second time, and it was a little easier to endure that strange feeling. It stopped and started again the third time. This time, I decided to relax and see what would happen. I then sensed the Lord's presence. He started speaking to me, and I was straining my ears to hear what He was saying. All I could make out was that the message was about children.

G) PRAYING FOR MORE FAITH.

I prayed in this dream, asking God to impart more faith to me, into my Spirit, to make me a stronger believer. As I prayed, I sensed in my Spirit a flash of lightning and I also sensed the "fear of the Lord" as well as sensing God's Holiness. I wish that it could have lasted longer, that I could bathe in His presence a little longer.

Chapter 5

Revelation Through Dreams

A) A Word from Heaven

I was standing on the side of the house where I grew up as a child. At the time of having this dream, that house did not exist anymore, it had been demolished years before. A gold object came floating down from the sky like a feather, not falling, affected by gravity, but descending as if an invisible hand was carrying it. I knew that it was a message from God. It landed (or was placed) between the bricks on the wall at the back of the house. In the front of the house, some people were lining up for food, but I did not know what the occasion was. I was not interested in food but was more interested in the "message" that came down from heaven.

I immediately wanted to go and retrieve the message, but I was restrained by the Holy Spirit not going there because the ground where the Word was delivered was "Holy Ground". I sensed the overwhelming presence of His Holiness and the fear of the Lord. I waited for the presence of God to depart from that place, and after it did, I hurried to retrieve the message to see what God was saying to me.

It was no longer gold, but I found a silver foil sealer with scripture references printed on it and a dark blue piece of gift paper with little golden crowns printed on it, as well as paper with different scripture verses written on it. The only scripture I could remember after waking up from the dream was, *"No flesh will glory in My presence".* I found that scripture later in 1 Corinthians 1 verse 29 *"That no flesh should glory in His presence"* (NKJV) Verse 30 to 31 *"But of Him you are in Christ Jesus who became for us wisdom from God, and righteousness and sanctification and redemption"- that as it is written "He who glories let Him glory in the Lord.* (Refer also to Jeremiah 9 verses 23 to 24)

For years, I have been perplexed that the Lord would send me such a peculiar message because I have never been someone who would boast about any accomplishments or anything for that matter. On the contrary, I prefer to remain obscure and unnoticed, but

God had a reason to communicate that message to me. However, my way of thinking about it was wrong because I reasoned with my natural mind.

Years after I had the dream, God revealed to me the meaning of the dream through scripture once again because I had asked Him, and I knew that He would reveal it to me one day. I found the answer in John chapter 6 verse 63 where Jesus says, *"It is the Spirit that gives life. The flesh profits nothing. The words that I speak to you are Spirit and they are life."*

Therefore, I perceived that the Lord was admonishing me as He deals with us through His Spirit because He has to allow our spiritual being to grow in the Word to be prepared for His heavenly kingdom. He also tells us in John chapter 3 that "Flesh and blood cannot inherit the Kingdom of God."

Also, if we consider the suffering and rejection of the prophets and apostles in the Bible, it also becomes evident that their flesh did not profit from their bringing their message to the people. Some of them were persecuted and killed for proclaiming God's message. God had dealt with them through the Spirit. Jesus says, "The flesh profits nothing. We are still living in a fallen world, and as followers of Christ, we need to endure the trials we must go through.

B) THE BRIGHT AND MORNING STAR/LIGHT OF THE WORLD

It was around 3 a.m. in the morning, and I found myself standing alone under a big tree. The whole town was asleep. I noticed a big, bright star in the East moving in my direction. As the star came closer, it shaped into a pillar of light. As it moved closer, it took on the shape of a huge cross. The Light kept moving closer and then I noticed that the arms of the cross shaped into the wings of a dove and then the whole shape of the cross took on the form of a big white dove. When it came right overhead, I saw that it was Jesus. All of these light forms shown to me in this dream represent the person of Jesus, who appeared right at the end above me. First the Morning Star, then the light of the world, then the dove indicating the Holy Spirit and finally Jesus Himself. He was looking down at the earth to see if the earth was ready to receive Him, and I knew in my heart that we were not ready. He moved across towards the West until He disappeared out of sight.

The Lord had been giving us many warnings to be ready for His return, but there will come a point in time when the warnings to humanity will stop, and that is the time when the door of the ark will close.

Revelation 22 verse 16: "I Jesus have sent My Angel to you to testify to you these things in the churches. I am the Root and the Offspring of David. The <u>Bright and Morning Star</u>."(NKJV)

We should also bear in mind that scripture warns us that He will come as a thief in the night. Therefore, we always need to be watchful and alert, for we do not know what hour He is coming.

C) Born to be King

When Pilate had asked Jesus if He was a King, Jesus answered him and said that He was a King and that He was born for that purpose, but that His Kingdom is not of this world.

So, in this dream, I found myself in this palace where there was a newborn baby boy dressed in blue, and I was asked by His mother, the Queen, to take Him for a walk, not with a stroller but just in my arms. Wherever I would walk with this baby, the people naturally knew that He was the newborn King, and they would bow down before and worship Him.

What I make of this dream is that the Lord wants people to know and understand about Jesus that it is He who was preordained to become the eternal King. It is He of whom the prophets have spoken. I marvel at how He revealed Himself to me in the ways that he did.

D) ANCIENT OF DAYS

My sister and I were together in a big room, like a courtroom, where I saw 3 Angels sitting on a stage on a throne. I asked her if she could see those angels, but she couldn't see them. I recognised the One in the middle as the "Ancient of Days", yet He did not appear to be old.

The Ancient of Days started speaking to me, and His voice was powerful and terrifying, like thunder. HE SPOKE WITH SUCH AUTHORITY!!!. "The authority He had spoken with was burned into my Spirit. The complete understanding of who He is - His Authority!) I could not understand the language that He had spoken in, and the sound of His voice was too powerful and frightening for me to endure. I shook my head, asking Him to stop speaking, as I could not stand in the power of His presence and endure the sound of His voice.

I so desired that I could have understood what the message was that He had spoken to me. I learned that "The Ancient of Days" is a term used to refer to God's eternity.

Daniel 7 verse 9 "I watched till thrones were put in place and the Ancient of Days was seated. His garment was white as wool, and the hair of His head was like pure wool. His throne was a fiery flame, its wheels a burning fire." (NKJV)

Daniel 7 verse 13 "I was watching in the night visions and behold, One like the Son of Man, coming with the clouds of heaven. He came to the Ancient of Days, and they brought Him near before Him."

Daniel 7 verse 22 " (MKJV)

Until the Ancient of Days came and a judgment was made in favour of the saints of the Most High and the time came for the saints to possess the Kingdom."(NKJV)

E) THE WIND AND THE WAVES OBEY

Alone on a barren stretch of beach, I noticed a Tsunami underway. I was running fast with the ocean on my left side. I needed to get to higher ground before the waves would crash onto the beach. There was a hill at the end of the beach, and I was hoping to make it there in time. Just as I reached higher ground, I found a woman at my feet who claimed to be Jesus. I did not just believe her, but I prayed to God to reveal to me if it was true what she had said. Just then, Jesus came around the corner on the hill, dressed in His linen garment, looking friendly. I had the sense that He was at last coming to inform me of my purpose and destiny. In that instant that He appeared and the mighty waves and the winds had "observed" the Master, the roaring ocean came to a freeze and the waters stopped in a heap ending in just a drop of water in mid-air. The sea did not move, nor did the wind continue to blow.

In Mathew 8 verse 26, Jesus rebuked the storm, but in my dream, the waves and the winds just froze at the sight of the Master. That was so awesome to me. Jesus is Lord over all of creation. The image in the dream was so vivid that if I were an artist, I would have painted that incredible scene that was shown to me in the dream.

At the rebuke of the sea and the calming of the storm, the disciples were astonished and asked among themselves, "Who is this that even the winds and the waves obey?" Matthew 8 verse 26 (NKJV)

I was amazed by this dream and humbled by Him revealing Himself to me in such a powerful way.

F) APPEARANCE OF AN EAGLE

Jesus appeared to me in the form of an eagle. The eagle had the face of a human, and somehow, I just knew that it was Jesus. He did not say anything to me. I recognised Him and said, "Jesus, I know it's you." I think that the Lord had put me to the test to see if I would recognise Him in the ways He had chosen to reveal Himself to me.

At the time of me having this dream, I did not realise the symbolic meaning of an eagle in relation to Christ. The eagle is often seen as a symbol of Christ, especially His resurrection and power and because of the eagle's strength and ability to soar high up into the sky and its excellent vision from great heights. The eagle's great visions are linked to Christ's divine vision to see beyond the physical reality on Earth.

It also represents the Lord's ascension to heaven and thereby the promise of eternal life after His resurrection.

Isaiah 41 verse 31 says that *"those who wait upon the Lord shall renew their strength. They shall mount up with wings like eagles. They shall run and not grow weary. They shall walk and not fa*int."

The Lord will reveal Himself to those who are asking Him.

In a separate vision, I saw a big brown eagle in flight high up in the sky. The vantage point from which I had observed the bird was from a point even higher up than where the eagle was in flight. The vision was so clear that I noticed every detail on its wings, white and black markings, and it amazed me that I could see the details on its wings with so much clarity.

G) BREAD OF LIFE

I was in a tent (tabernacle) with some children and I was in the front section of the tent. More children were in the back of the tent being very noisy. Jesus then appeared among us in the front section with a plate of broken bread/manna, (a small round substance as described in Exodus 16 verse 14). He offered each person to take a piece of bread. When He came to me, I asked Him if that was the Bread of Life and without saying it in words, He affirmed that it indeed was the bread of life. I took mine but realised that I had taken two pieces. I then said to Him, "Sorry, Jesus, I took two. He answered me again without speaking words; *"Even better".*

I ate the bread and it tasted unlike anything I had eaten before. It was a beautiful taste, sweet like honey.

Scripture references that refer to the Bread of Life (NKJV)

Deuteronomy 8 verse 3" So He humbled you, allowed you to hunger, and fed you with Manna which you did not know that He might make you know that man shall not live

SOPHIA R. BAILEY

by bread alone, but man lives by every word that proceeds from the mouth of God."(NKJV)

Psalm 119 verse 103:" How sweet are Your words to my taste. Sweeter than honey to the mouth." (NKJV)

Jeremiah 15 verse 16: "Your words were found, and I ate them and Your words were to me the joy and rejoicing of my heart. For I am called by Your Name Lord, God Almighty."(NKJV)

John 6 verse 33: "For the bread of God is He who comes down from heaven and gives life to the world."(NKJV)

His Word is the bread of life that we must eat in order to receive eternal life. Jesus is the Word.

The meaning of this dream is self-explanatory through scripture alone. God had shown me that because I was hungry for His Word, He willingly made His Word known to me. I fed on His Word because I desired to understand it and to be obedient to Him. As in the dream, His Word was sweet like honey to my taste.

H) LIVING WATERS

I was standing on the bank of a very wide river. I am drinking from this river and the water was amazingly refreshing to me. It quenched my thirst and I just could not drink enough of this water.

John 4 verse 14: Whoever drinks of the water that I shall give him will never thirst, But the water that I shall give him I will become to Him a fountain of water, springing up into everlasting life." (NKJV)

Psalm 36 verse 8 they are abundantly satisfied with the fullness of Your house. And You give them drink from the River of Your pleasures."

The living waters rising up in a believer is the presence of the Spirit of God who dwells in the hearts of man.

I) Hidden Treasures

I was on my stomach, sliding down a sand dune in the desert, when I noticed a rock sticking out from beneath the sand in front of me. I tried to clear the sand with my hands and noticed that I was on top of the roof of a house. This house was buried under the desert sand. The next thing I knew, I was standing in front of the house with two "officials" accompanying me. It was an ancient building, built from stone. I was not allowed to enter without permission. One of the authorized persons unlocked the door and I found myself in the kitchen area. There, I beheld untold treasures and valuables from ancient times. The room was filled with it – jewellery, precious stones, paintings, artefacts, gold and silver vessels – all kinds of treasures. I gasped in disbelief. I also noticed two green closed doors leading from the passage, but I knew not to enter through those doors. It was not the right time to enter through them because I understood that there would be even more valuable treasures behind those doors.

God has made known to me that these treasures I had dreamed of are the treasures of His Word and of Christ, who gives knowledge, wisdom and eternal life.

I found such beautiful confirmation of this truth in different verses in the Bible, especially the treasure of Christ Jesus, for it is written in *Colossians 2 verses 2-3, "that in God, both the Father and of Christ is hidden all the treasures of wisdom and of knowledge." (NKJV)*

Matthew 6 verse 21: "For where your treasure is, your heart will be also." (NKJV)

Psalm `119 verse 162: "I rejoice at Your Word as one who found great treasures." (NKJV)

Isaiah 45 verse 3: "I will give you the treasures of darkness and hidden riches of secret places, that you may know that I the Lord, who call you by your name, am the God of Israel." (NKJV)

Christ is <u>my</u> treasure and <u>my</u> riches.

J) THE ROCK

The waves of the ocean headed in my direction and when I saw it coming, I tried to run away, but there was nowhere to escape because the mountain was on the other side. I started climbing out of the rock to escape the waves, but the waves came and engulfed me.

"The Lord is my Rock and my fortress."

In another dream, flood waters were coming down the mountain and cascading down the rocks. We had our house built on a high rock, and all the water was just flowing around our house. We did not fear, as our house was built on the Rock. (Jesus Christ – our Rock and our Salvation).

Matthew 7 verse 24 -25 "Therefore, whoever hears these sayings of Mine and does them, I will liken him to a wise man who builds his house upon a rock. And the rains descended, and the floods came, and the winds blew and beat on that house and it did not fall for it was founded upon the rock." (Jesus CHRIST) (NKJV)

K) THE WARRIOR KING

This was a vision I had received as I was thinking about prophetic events unfolding.

I "saw" the Lord riding on His white horse, draped with a red mantle and a golden crown on His head. The armies of heaven were following *Him*.

In Revelation 19, scripture lays out this vision beautifully:"

Revelation 19 verses 11-15. "Now I saw heaven opened and behold a white horse. And He who sat on him was called Faithful and True, and in righteousness He judges and makes war. His eyes were like a flame of fire, and on His head were many crowns. He had a Name that no one knew except Himself. He was clothed in a robe dipped in blood and His Name is called "THE WORD OF GOD." And the armies in heaven clothed in fine linen, white and clean, followed Him on white horses. Now out of His mouth goes a sharp sword that with it He should strike the nations. And He Himself will rule them with a rod of iron. He Himself treads the wine press and fierceness of Almighty God."(NKJV)

L) A STERN KING

We were in a big building together, my sisters and I, when I saw a King sitting on His throne with a very stern countenance. I was standing in the doorway of the hall, at an angle where I could see into an adjacent room. There, one of my sisters was holding up a golden plaque on a long stick with a depiction of the stone tablets of the Law and very interesting symbols and language engraved on it. I was gazing at this inscription and my gaze shifted between the message and the King sitting on His throne as if I was trying to make some connection between the King and the message that was engraved on the plaque. At that point, He was not facing my way. Then I noticed the letter "J" appearing from the top to the bottom of the plaque among the symbols and the depiction of the Old Testament stone Tablets with more inscriptions on it, which I had assumed was the Ten Commandments, written by the finger of God on the two tablets of stone.

When I deciphered the letter J and that it meant Jesus, I decided to approach the king boldly and to let Him know that I had perceived the Letter J to indicate the Name of Jesus and that I knew that He was Jesus – that He was the King. When mentioning to Him my observation and revelation of the inscriptions on the plaque pointing to Him, the stern countenance changed into a sheer warm, friendly demeanour and He seemed very joyful that I had recognized Him as Jesus the Savior King. I assumed that it probably was just a test I had to undergo to test my faith and discernment of the God of Abraham, Isaac and Jacob.

Isaiah 65 verse 1 "I was sought by those who did not ask for Me. I was found by those who did not seek Me. I said "Here I am, here I am." To a nation that was not called by My Name."(NKJV)

I couldn't help but notice a correlation between this dream and the vision I had received from the Lord years before - the vision about the book. On the cover of the book I saw, there was also a depiction of the stone tablets with the commandments engraved on them in an ancient language. It seems to me that God's intentions were to show me the connection between the old and the new covenants, making all of us one in Christ.

M) EVERY KNEE WILL BOW

In this dream, I saw a huge asteroid falling from the sky onto a city. When it hit the city, clouds, debris and smoke filled the sky, explosions rocked the city and people were running for their lives – it was chaos. Then I heard the voice of the Lord, saying: *"As I live, every knee will bow."* I later found this scripture in Romans 14:11 (NKJV)

N) THE LAMB

In this dream, I saw myself carrying a pure snow-white, spotless little lamb in my arms, with a bright white light shining onto the lamb. In my Spirit, I knew it represented the Lamb of God spoken of in the book of Revelation.

John 1 verse 29 "The next day John saw Jesus coming towards him and said" Behold the Lamb of God Who takes away the sin of the world." (NKJV)

Revelation 5 verse 12 "Worthy is the Lamb who was slain, to receive power and riches and wisdom and strength and honour and glory and blessings." (NKJV)

I felt blessed that God allowed me to carry the white little lamb in my arms even if it was just in a dream.

O) THE FIRE OF GOD

A Jewish man and I were standing in the lobby of some auditorium. There, in the lobby, we saw a fire burning. This fire was not like a normal fire burning with orange flames, but it was just one big white light coated by an unknown substance/covering. The Jewish man tells me not to look at the fire as it was the fire of God and if we dare to look at It, our eyes might be blinded. I ignored his warning and looked at the fire but found that it didn't harm my eyes at all. We had also received a message that the ground where the fire was located was Holy Ground, so we left the auditorium.

The interpretation in my own heart is that the dream speaks about the veil that is still covering the eyes of Jewish people who haven't found Messiah yet, and therefore, it is my prayer that the time will come when God will remove the veil from their eyes as scripture promises, so that they would recognize who Yeshua is.

Since I can remember, I have always had a burden for the Jewish people, as I understood that they are the people of the God, the people of the Bible, and that God had blinded their eyes in part until the fullness of the Gentiles, then "All Israel" will be saved as scripture says.

Romans 11 verse 25 "For I do not desire brethren that you should be ignorant of the mystery, lest you should be wise in your own opinion that blindness in part has happened to Israel until the fullness of the gentiles has come in and so all Israel will be saved," (NKJV)

P) THE PEACEMAKER

It happened that I found myself in war-torn Syria, people running to and fro among the collapsed and ruined buildings, looking for survivors, that I noticed Jesus approaching, and He seemed to be in a hurry. Somehow, I was lying flat on my stomach on the ground, wanting to speak with Him, but he hurriedly passed by. I could only touch the hem of His garment. I received the assurance from Him in my spirit (without words being spoken) that He would be back to speak with me, but at that time, He had urgent matters to attend to, to bring about peace to the region.

Jesus is referred to as the Prince of Peace, as described in Isaiah 9 verse 6. Many people reason that He cannot be that Prince of peace that the Bible talks about, since when He came into the world, He didn't bring peace according to the world's perception of peace, but the peace He brought is the peace that reigns in the human heart, having received the remission of sin and being reconciled to God.

Ephesians 2 verse 14 "For He Himself is our peace who has made both one and has broken down the middle wall of separation. (NKJV)

Q) RESURRECTION POWER

It was night time and I was walking over a bridge. There were a few other people walking that road as well, but they did not notice what I had seen. There, on the bridge, I noticed a body wrapped in sackcloth and for some reason, I knew that it was Jesus's body wrapped in the sackcloth. There was some kind of communication from the body (I don't remember what) but I answered Him and said, "Jesus, only You have the power to raise Yourself up, nobody else can raise You. I repeated this three times and Immediately after the third time, the dead body rose and transformed itself into a body of light and He stood upright, looking radiant. Once again, I recognised the Lord while He was trying to "disguise" Himself and for me to see if I would recognise Him.

I took notice of this related scripture years after the dream in *John 10 verse 17-18 "Therefore My Father loves Me, because I lay down My life that I may take it again. No one takes it from Me, I lay it down of Myself. I have power to lay it down and power to take it again. This command I have received from My Father." (NKJV)*

Although I have read this scripture many times before, I only made this connection between the dream and the scripture as I was busy writing the book.

Also, in *John 11 verse 25 Jesus says, "I Am the resurrection and the life, He who believes in me though he may die he shall live. And whoever lives and believe in me shall never die." (NKJV)*

CHAPTER 6
PURSUING WATERS

A) THE WAVES OF THE SEA

I had different dreams in which the waves from the ocean would follow me to engulf me. In this particular dream, I was walking on the beach. I saw the waves coming closer to the beach where I was and I kept trying to get out of the way. The further I moved away, the more the waves followed me. The waves were growing huge in size and the foam at the crest of the waves formed huge white pillars extending higher up into the air right above me. I took a path leading away from the beach to my sister's house close by to escape the waves but it kept following me. Just as I got safely inside after closing the door, a gigantic wave engulfed the house but I was secure and dry inside the house.

I did not understand at the time that the waves following me and other structures of water were the Holy Spirit pursuing me.

B) WATERED FROM THE CLOUDS

My siblings and I were sitting on the rocks, watching the waves. It wasn't the normal coastal sea but a sea on dry land. I noticed a big wave coming and I started running away without warning them. Just as I was "out of the way ", a big wave washed over them sitting on the rocks and because I had escaped the water, the Hand of God poured water onto me directly from the clouds and I was soaking wet from head to toe. I found it so hilarious I started laughing uncontrollably, being filled with joy. I laughed myself awake and still continued laughing after I had awakened because the "joy of the Lord" was still welling up inside of me.

In Isaiah 44 verse 3 I found this scripture that revealed the meaning of the dream to me, *"I will pour water on him who is thirsty and floods on dry ground, I will pour My Spirit on your descendants and My blessings on your offspring."* (NKJV)

Proverbs 1 verse 23 *"Turn at My rebuke. Surely, I will pour out My Spirit on you. I WILL MAKE MY WORDS KNOWN TO YOU."(NKJV)*

C) THE RIVER OF LIFE

I was walking upstream along the banks of a broad river. I noticed an unusual wave in the middle of the river. The next thing I knew, the wave that I had seen came right over from the middle of the river to where I was walking and washed over me. I also found it hilarious as I got soaking wet from that one wave. Once again, I was filled with the joy of the Lord as His Spirit came washing over me and I could hardly keep in my laughter.

D) THE FOUNTAIN OF LIFE

My friend and I were sitting next to a fountain, where the water was gushing up from the deep straight up into the air. The water gushing up suddenly changed direction. The water formed a curved angle, passing my friend and pouring right onto me. It seemed to have a will of its own in that it wanted to engulf and submerge me only and not my friend.

Psalm 36 verse 9 "For with You is the fountain of life. In Your light we see light." (NKJV)

Revelation 21 verse 6 "And He said to me "It is done. I Am the Alpha and the Omega, the beginning and the end. I will give the fountain of the water of life freely to him who thirsts." (NKJV)

E) RAINS FROM HEAVEN

Here I was just walking alone in a rain shower, feeling refreshed while being drenched in the rain.

Isaiah 55 verse 10-11 "For as the rain comes down and the snow from heaven and do not return there, but water the earth and makes it bring forth bud, that it gives seed to the sower and bread to the eater, so shall My Word be that goes forth from My Mouth. It shall not return to Me void but it shall accomplish that which I please. And it shall prosper in the thing for which I sent it."

F) MOUNTAIN STREAM

I crossed a stream where the bridge was made of stepping stones leading to the foot of a mountain on the other side of the brook. I received a message in my spirit that only people who want to climb the mountain could cross the stream or else you might slip and fall into the water and be carried away by it. I crossed the stream willingly and effortlessly and found myself at the foot of the mountain with a cool, gentle mountain stream cascading over me. I was just standing there, with the water cascading over my body being refreshed by those cool and living waters, yet I did not get soaked by the water.

CHAPTER 7
MORE DREAMS

A) FISHING FOR JESUS

At the break of dawn, I found myself standing alone on the beach with a fishing rod in my hand that just appeared out of nowhere. I threw the line into the water to catch a fish. Then I noticed a sun in the sky and I was puzzled by it because it was still dawn and the sun hadn't risen yet. I then realised that the sun shining in the sky was the Lord Himself. "Good morning, Lord, how are You?" I asked as a matter of fact. It didn't take long for the fish to bite and I pulled out the rod. Out of the water came a fish and a white dove – it seemed that they came out "willingly" if I can put it that way, because the fish did not try to get back into the water, neither did the dove try to fly away. While I pulled the line out of the water, the scripture verse in Matthew 17 verse 27 *came into my spirit where the Lord Jesus instructed the disciples to catch a fish that will have a coin in it's mouth which will have to be used to pay the taxes.* (NKJV)

B) GOING TO MOUNT ZION

We were going up a high mountain, and on top of the mountain, a lot of people were lining up to receive rewards, but it was only the people lining up on the right – the people on the left were just standing there, looking lost and envious, that they could not receive any rewards. The meaning of the dream was obvious to me. I knew that it related to the saved and the unsaved; Let the reader also see this as an invitation to come to the Mountain of the Lord, Mount Zion, to dwell with the Lord forever.

Isaiah 2 verse 2 "Now it shall come to pass that the mountain of the Lord's house shall be established on top of the mountains. And it shall be exalted above the hills and all nations shall flow to it."(NKJV)

C) THE MOUNTAIN TOP

A long line of people was approaching a high mountain, snaking through the valleys to get to the top of the mountain and on top of the mountain, where the line of people ended, the number eight appeared. Eight represents new beginnings which I interpret as the New life in Christ.

In another dream, I saw some people coming up to the top of the mountain. I was already on the mountain and watching the people ascending,

The mountain top in itself represents to me new beginnings. People are invited to come to the mountain of the Lord through Jesus Christ, our Savior. The Bible also speaks about His Holy Hill, where the saints can live an everlasting life through Him, who gives eternal life.

D) THE HIGHWAY TO HOLINESS

In late July or early August, some years ago, I had a dream where I was driving alone in a car on a highway leading into a city when I noticed the billboards overhead showing the directions and names of the exits and I saw that the next exit approaching was called "AV BOULEVARD". That was the dream.

As I was contemplating the meaning of the dream the next day, I remembered that the name "Av" was the name of a Hebrew month. I decided to google the name and found that AV literally means "Father" and that it was indeed the name of a month on the Hebrew calendar. I remembered that there is a scripture in Isaiah about "The Highway of Holiness", but I was just not sure where in Isaiah it is found. I read through the book of Isaiah and found it in Chapter 35.

Moreover, exactly a year later also in late July or early August, I had the following dream. I was walking down a road when I noticed, in some distance, a bow of white flowers spanned across the road. In front of the flowers was a pillar of light emanating white light towards me. As I was still approaching the Light, it came swirling towards me, surrounding me and enveloping me like in an embrace. I noticed that the light appeared to be like a white mist.

Needless to say, when I read Isaiah 35 verses 8 to 10, I realised that God once again just taught me scripture for my spiritual growth.

Isaiah 35 verse 8-10: *"A highway shall be there and a road and it shall be called the Highway of Holiness. The unclean shall not pass over it but it shall be for others. Whoever walks this road, although a fool, shall not go astray. No lion shall be there nor shall any ravenous beast be on it. They shall not be found there. BUT THE REDEEMED SHALL WALK THERE AND THE RANSOMED OF THE LORD SHALL RETURN AND COME TO ZION WITH SINGING. WITH EVERLASTING JOY ON THEIR HEADS. THEY SHALL OBTAIN GLADNESS AND SORROW AND SIGHING SHALL FLEE FROM THEM." (NKJV)*

The "unclean" In this scripture simply implies that those who haven't been washed by the blood of the

Lamb will not walk on the road that leads to everlasting life.

"Today is the day of Salvation", so I urge everyone to call on the Name of the Lord. Only through His blood we can be washed clean and be saved for eternal life.

E) FLOWERS RAINING DOWN FROM HEAVEN

Some people gathered together in front of some church buildings of different denominations. I was there also, talking to people about Jesus. Some of the people chose to come with me, to go and worship the Lord, so we went to a public park, where everything was so beautiful and green, the grass, the trees and the plants. We started worshipping God, and it started raining flowers – white and purple flowers until it filled up the ground and looked like a tapestry.

It was indicative to me that the Lord was pleased with the praises and worship of His people.

F) WAVES OF LIGHT

We were gathered at a family member's house when waves and explosions of light came forth from the sky upon us. I ordered everyone to lie down flat on the ground and I felt that the glory of the Lord had been poured upon us. I prayed God would manifest more of His Glory upon us.

G) ASCENDING TOWARDS THE LIGHT (MINORA}

In this dream, I am ascending, and there is a golden Minora above me. I know no other details about this dream and also do not yet understand its meaning other than that which could represent Jesus as the Light of the World.

H) VISION OF AN ASTEROID

I had a vision of an asteroid coming down to Earth with a long tail. Afterwards, I saw the Hand of God reaching out to me from the clouds to pull me to safety. This might also be rapture-related, as I see this as a way in which God will save us when trouble hits the earth.

I) CALLING ON HIS NAME (HEAVEN IS MY THRONE)

I woke up from a dream in which I was being attacked by a demon for reciting a scripture verse. I woke up trying to say the words, but all I heard was a strange mumbling coming from my mouth. I knew that I was quoting scripture, but the words were not audible and clear. My husband also heard me mumbling. The words I was trying to utter were, *"Heaven is My throne and the earth is My footstool. Where is the house that you will build Me and where is the place of my rest?"* This scripture is found in Isaiah 66 verse 1. The evil entity was trying to close my mouth, so I could not utter those words.

J) STAR PAINTING

It was night time and I was busy painting a portrait of the starry sky. The gold-coloured stand-up frame was already in place, yet there was no canvas on the frame, but I was doing the painting. I put my foot through the frame and to my delight the picture that I was busy painting changed into the real starry sky. When I would bring my foot out of the frame, it would turn back into just a painting. I repeated it a few times and would again see the real starry sky when I put my foot through the frame.

K) A SILVER FISH

A big silver fish had washed out onto the shore from the ocean. There were no people on the beach, except myself, looking at this fish stranded in front of a beach house.

I did not make anything out of this dream, but it stuck in my mind. A few weeks after I had the dream, I came across a documentary in which archaeologists have uncovered a mosaic-tiled floor in Israel dating back to early Christianity. They had found inscriptions and fish icons in the mosaic floor tiles in the Greek language. It is said that the fish symbol (ichtus in Greek) is an acronym for Jesus Christ. I found this discovery very interesting, however, I still did not understand the symbolism of the stranded fish if the fish represents Jesus. But I do know that the fish symbol was the Christian symbol for the early church.

L) SWINGS FROM THE CLOUDS

I was swinging through the air on huge swings with ropes coming down from the sky. I was swinging throughout the world over different mountain ranges, which were very impressive, looking on from a great height. At times, I could swing effortlessly and other times, I had to hold on for dear life so as not to loosen my grip and tumble down to earth.

M) SILVERY GLOW

In this dream, I was walking on a road when a stranger came up to me and remarked that there was something weird about me. She moved her hand across my face and said that there was a silvery glow around my face as if she wanted to feel what it was.

N) 3500-MILE JOURNEY

I was to embark on a journey of 3500 miles (or km). I was shown an aerial view of the map that I was to travel. The map was dark but I noticed mountain ranges below and the road snaking through hills and valleys. The road looked like a graph drawn with a pencil in yellow. I did research to see what the number 3500 represents in the Hebrew language. It showed that the number 3500 means "remnant", or "what is left", or "a string attached". I realised that God was exactly showing me that He could still use me for His purpose even if so many years of my life were wasted.

O) DREAMS OF MY SPIRIT BODY

I saw myself, my "spirit body", being radiant, young and emanating light. I had this dream twice. At first, I didn't recognize myself, but afterwards, I was just being "shown" what we would look like in our newly resurrected bodies. I also saw myself lying on my bed, looking like a "Big white bird with wings."

Chapter 8
The Calling

A) MESSAGE IN THE SKY

In this dream, I was about to enter a subway at a station when I noticed a message written in the sky with white clouds. The message simply read: 1 Cor 14: 1.

I woke up immediately after the dream and I

took my Bible to see what the verse says. This is what is written:

"Pursue love and desire spiritual gifts, but especially that you may prophesy."(NKJV) In another translation, it reads: "that you may proclaim God's message.".

I thought that it was an amazing message from God and I wondered why He would give me that particular message. I still did not understand that the Lord was calling me for an assignment. The thought also came to my mind that I was no prophet, I had no desire to be one, and I didn't have the gift of prophecy. I just left it at that, for I had no idea what God wanted me to do. I kept a journal of my dreams, hoping to receive some revelation one day.

B) Word from Jeremiah 1

In 1999, I was training at a Mission School to become a full-time missionary. By then, I had the desire to serve God in a full-time capacity. I wanted to change the whole world for Jesus, but unfortunately, it didn't work out that way.

It was our summer break and my friend and I were waiting at the station for the bus to arrive. We were just chatting away (I had my Bible on my lap). The bible slid off my lap and I noticed that it fell open at the first chapter of Jeremiah. I picked it up, not thinking anything about it and put it back on my lap. About half an hour later -with my Bible still on my lap, the same thing happened then once again, the Bible fell open at Jeremiah Chapter 1. It still did not raise any "alarm bells" in my mind. I simply picked it up and put it back on my lap. I must just add here that there was no bookmark at that chapter or anywhere in the Bible - it was a new Bible and it didn't even have any creases on the pages.

The bus arrived, we boarded the bus and departed. About an hour later, after our departure (the two of us still chatting away), for a third time, the Bible slid off my lap at Jeremiah chapter 1. This time, I took notice and a light went off in my head. I picked it up and said to my friend, "What is it with Jeremiah 1? Maybe God wants to say something to me." I then decided that I needed to pay attention and read what God wanted to say. I only read it later after my friend fell asleep. I was astounded when I read in verse 3 (that is where my eyes focused first and the message spoke directly to my spirit.), " *Before I formed you in the womb, I knew you. Before you were born, I sanctified you. I ordained you a prophet to the nations.*"(NKJV)

I was puzzled as to why God would give me a word like that. I did not see myself as a prophet, I did not feel like a prophet, but most of all, I did not have the gift of prophecy, or so I thought. My idea of a prophet is a man like Moses, Daniel, Jeremiah, Zechariah and all the prophets in the Bible. I did not understand at the time what God had meant by that – I would only understand much later in my life what God had ordained for me.

During the time of my training as a missionary, I found out that there were Prophetic Schools where people who wanted to become prophets could go and receive training. In my opinion, a prophet is chosen and anointed by God, who fills them with His Spirit. I did not think that a prophet could be trained by human institutions. This is just my opinion.

I put this word to the back of my mind, thinking that God will in due time, reveal His plans and purpose for my life.

C) A GOLDEN PEN

I dreamed that a golden pen was floating down from above, coming my way as if carried by an unseen hand from the sky. I was sitting at the back of a building flat on the ground with my legs outstretched. The pen landed (or was placed) in my right hand. A bright light shone from above right onto the pen in my hand, highlighting it. I noticed the initials J.C. (Jesus Christ) engraved on the pen in this light shining from above. When I awoke, I knew that it was a reminder from the Lord and that He had "given" me a mandate to write the book that He had shown me in the vision years before.

I have wasted a number of years before writing this book and here the Lord reminded me of the promise that I had made to Him. Sad to say, I still did not proceed with the instructions as I still did not understand what the message of the book should be. There were also many distractions in my life and the cares of life began to lead me down a different path.

However, the dreams continued and as time passed, I began to understand more and more what the Lord wanted me to do. It was a slow process, while my spiritual growth sometimes became stagnant.

D) ARISE AND SHINE

In this dream, I was reading from Isaiah 60 and my spirit was greatly impacted by these awe-inspiring words.

Verse 3 – 5: *"Arise shine for your light has come. And the glory of the Lord has risen upon you. For behold the darkness shall cover the earth and deep darkness the people. But the Lord shall arise over you and His glory will be seen upon you. The gentiles shall come to your light and kings to the brightness of your glory."* (NKJV)

How beautiful this prophecy is and how promising it is to those of us who haven't known the God of Israel, the true and Living God. He had been mindful of all the peoples of the world from the beginning but chose to make Himself known to His people, Israel first and then to the nations. It is an awesome prophecy and I delight in feeding on His Word daily to refresh and feed my spirit man.

I believe this scripture talks about the rapture to which all believers are looking forward to.

E) WHITE BUTTERFLIES

In this precious, beautiful dream, a lot of white butterflies descended upon me as if I were a flower bush. They just came to sit all over me. It gave me a very special feeling and I thought that it also indicated that the Holy Spirit was working in me.

F) WHITE BIRDS

A lot of white birds came flying and landed upon me. At first, I panicked because I wasn't sure what it meant, but I was soon comforted by the Holy Spirit that they wouldn't harm me in any way but that it was once again a sign of His presence upon me.

G) WHITE DOVES

A number of white doves were following me as I was riding on a bicycle. They came down and sat on my shoulders while I was riding on. This time, I was not afraid, but I knew that the Lord was with me and I actually enjoyed their company.

H) PREPARATION

I was sitting in a dark place with a few other ladies. We just had to sit there and wait as we were being prepared as brides for a bridegroom. I did not know who the bridegroom/s would be and was just sitting there, waiting with the others. While waiting, a flame of fire went upwards from me to God. I received the impression in the dream that it was a sacrifice that was acceptable to Him, hence the fire going up from me. However, I cannot say what the sacrifice was other than my "broken heart and contrite spirit." *"The sacrifices of God are a broken spirit. A broken spirit and a contrite heart. These, you will not despise, O Lord." Psalm 51 verse 17 (NKJV)*

Psalm 18 verse 28 "For You will light my lamp. The Lord my God, will enlighten my darkness." (NKJV)

I) VISION OF A GOLDEN MANTLE

I saw the hand of God draping a golden mantle over my shoulders. I sensed God speaking words of encouragement to me. The next day, I saw a friend of mine who had placed an ad on Facebook inviting people to join a teaching session about the spiritual meaning of a mantle and what the different colours represent. I did some research and discovered that the meaning of a mantle is the gift of prophecy, a task God has bestowed upon whoever He pleases.

CHAPTER 9
RAPTURE DREAMS

A) SUSPENDED IN MID-AIR

Awaiting the Rapture, Jesus and I were suspended in mid-air while He was holding me by my right hand. We were expecting to see Him coming for us while, at the same time, He was with me, holding my hand. We looked down to the earth below and we saw figures coming forth from the ground. He told me that it was the "dead rising", as it is written in the scriptures.

After He had said that, everything disappeared before my eyes, and the whole scene turned blue. Everything had just vanished. I woke up shaken because the encounter had felt so real.

Thessalonians 4 verse 16: For the Lord Himself will descend from heaven with a shout with the voice of an archangel and with the trumpet call of God. And the dead in Christ shall rise first." (NKJV)

B) Wedding tables

This was a dream in which I was shown rows of tables set for a wedding and the tables stretched on forever.

Revelation 19 verse 7 "Let us be glad and rejoice and give Him Glory for the marriage supper of the Lamb has come and His wife (church) has made herself ready."(NKJV)

C) People dressed in white

In different dreams, I saw many people all dressed in white, getting ready for the rapture. In one of the dreams, people were joyful and busy with preparations for the wedding feast. Some of them didn't know what to wear to the wedding.

D) Saints leaving on trains

My husband and I were at a train station where a lot of people were gathered to leave for the rapture. Some people had already boarded the train and were waving goodbye to those left behind. The excitement among those leaving was unbelievable. I was shouting, "Jesus is coming, Jesus is coming." The two of us decided to warn others before we would board the train. We ran to a church building close by where a service was about to begin. When we got there, the worship team was just about ready for the worship session. We went to the worship leaders and told them that the rapture was about to take place and asked that they make an announcement in the service for people to get ready.

This dream reminded me of the parable of the 10 virgins. Five of them were wise and the other five were foolish. The foolish ones had no oil in their lamps, while the five wise virgins had their lamps filled. The oil is the Holy Spirit by which we must be filled to be saved.

Some Christians are not even aware that there is a teaching in the Bible about the rapture because they are not being taught this in church. Neither do they study nor read their Bibles for themselves.

Revelation 16 verse 15 "Behold I am coming as a thief in the night. Blessed is he who watches and keeps his garment, lest he walks naked and they see his shame." (NKJV)

E) AUDIENCE WITH THE KING

A bride and a bridegroom, both dressed in their white wedding attire, had an audience with a King in His chambers. The place looked out of the ordinary, with very rare wooden furniture – almost like a courtroom, just with much more grandeur. I knew that certain ceremonies were executed, but only the one that I mentioned here I could remember. I was watching this scene unfolding from a vantage point up higher, yet at the same time, I was also the bride. The King was dressed in His white linen garment with a golden crown on His head and a sceptre in His hand. The King stretched out His sceptre towards the bride and the bridegroom. They too had their own sceptres in their hands and when the King held out His sceptre towards them, they did the same and also stretched out their sceptres toward the King, The three sceptres made contact and a message was communicated to us by the King (even if no words were spoken.} The message I received in my spirit was that the time had come for all the prophetic events written about in the Bible to be fulfilled. The fact that all three of them held out the sceptres meant that they all agreed that it is indeed time for the fulfilment of prophetic events, which we can already see unfolding in the world today.

After praying and contemplating the meaning of this dream, it became clear to me that the King represented God the Father. The bridegroom is, of course, Jesus Christ and the bride is the church, hence me representing the bride. I was so excited and full of expectations about this dream – it gave me renewed hope that we could be going home soon.

Revelation 19 verse 9 "Then He said to me, write, "blessed are those who are called to the marriage supper of the Lamb."(NKV)

F) Multitudes gathering

A multitude of people were gathered on the seashore, awaiting the rapture. It was twilight and the sea was very calm, with the gentle waves softly spilling onto the beach. There was a holy hush in the air covering the multitude as they waited. Then suddenly, all the people fell on their knees to the ground, weeping and worshipping Jesus. They got back onto their feet after a while and just continued waiting. Then I saw some object coming from the sky (I assumed it represented an angel), descending onto the people to put God's mark of ownership upon everyone present there. The ocean represents the nations of the world and It is written in Isaiah, *"the nations will come into your inheritance."*

G) Train departing

Another one of my "train departing" dreams was when I was watching from a vantage point a train pulling in at the station. The train was filled with people leaving for the rapture. I sensed a huge unseen crowd all around me in the air, also watching the train. The train stopped to allow more people to board, but nobody else boarded and one person disembarked.

H) ANGELS TO THE RESCUE

In this dream, flood waters were carrying people away and they were screaming for help. I saw the Angels of God coming through the clouds, reaching out their arms and pulling out the people of God from the raging waters to safety.

I) A BRIDEGROOM

I dreamed of a young bridegroom wearing a silver suit, being ready for his wedding. He looked excited and was just putting the finishing touches on his shoes.

I gathered that this bridegroom represents Jesus preparing to come for His bride, ready at any time.

CHAPTER 10
END TIMES DREAMS AND WARNINGS

A) POURING OUT HIS SPIRIT

In this dream, I saw a bottle up in the sky, moving by itself through the air. The bottle was tilted down with its mouth at the bottom and water running out of it while it was floating through the sky. As soon as the drops of water made contact with the air, every drop would turn into a white dove and the doves would fly in all directions. More and more doves manifested from the water that came out of the bottle. At first, I tried to count them, but it was impossible as they just kept coming and flying away out of site. It was such an amazing sight to behold, even if it was just a dream.

At the time that I had this dream, I didn't know the meaning of it, but I soon discovered that the dream was telling me about prophecy in scripture. In Job 38 verse

37 it is written: "Who can number the clouds by wisdom and who can pour out the bottles of heaven."(NKJV)

Also, In Joel 2 verse 28 it is written: *"And it will come to pass afterwards, that I will pour out My Spirit on all flesh. Your sons and your daughters shall prophesy and your old men shall dream dreams and you young men shall see visions. And also on my menservants and My maidservants, I will pour out my Spirit in those days."(NKJV)*

B) Time stopped

It was about 7 o'clock in the morning and I was on my way to work. I noticed that time had stopped as I was looking at my watch. I also noticed that everyone else in the vicinity looked at their watches, and we were all looking up to the sky for an answer. Then we saw the animals that were in Noah's ark approaching from behind the clouds and disappearing into the air.

This dream left me puzzled as the only explanation I could think of was that the Lord may have conveyed to us that it was the beginning of the time that He had equated to the days of Noah in the Bible.

C) Dream of Chemical spray

In the mid-nineties, I had this dream in which I was flying with another person, an Air Force pilot in a plane that sprayed some chemical substance onto the earth below. People were running indoors for safety because the spray was burning their skins and babies were getting sick. The pilot of the plane told me that I must be a witness to the things that were happening. At the time I had received this dream, I had no idea of chemtrails or any such things happening today.

I realised that God had given me another prophetic dream without me having any knowledge about it.

D) BLACK RAINS

The rain coming down was black and it was burning people. They all ran for shelter and cover. I thought that it may just speak of an end-time scenario.

E) BLOOD RIVER ON THE MOON

The full moon was bright and bigger than usual. There was a river of blood flowing on the moon and it was visible with the naked eye from the earth. I can only say that it might also refer to an end-time scenario.

F) REVEALING OF THE ANTI-CHRIST.

The Anti-Christ was about to be revealed. People were gathering at a shopping mall to see his identity. There was a huge television screen just outside the centre, where everyone could watch the event. When it was time for the show to start, instead of him being revealed, the footage of a huge red dragon appeared on the screen. While waiting to see who he is, the people gathered there received word that the time for revealing his identity had not yet arrived.

G) AS IT WAS IN THE DAYS OF NOAH

On my left, there was a high mountain, water cascading over the rocks and some people were gathered together to watch the events unfold. Out of the ground, water came bubbling up from the ground and the waters from above and below started filling up the ground. We were watching in amazement as we realised what it meant. A woman standing close to me started quoting scripture together in one voice saying, *"AS IT WAS IN THE DAYS OF NOAH SO SHALL IT BE IN THE DAYS OF THE SON OF MAN."*

H) FIVE STARS FALLING

A bright star shooting across the sky from the west to the east hit the ocean and the result of this was that the water would shoot up into the air, forming a fiery crown. God's voice then thundered from heaven, speaking a Word. *(I can't say for sure whether it was a commandment or if it was another kind of warning, but God had spoken.)* This happened five times that a star fell from heaven, a fiery crown formed and God's voice thundered a commandment. People witnessing this were terrified of the voice of God. It stopped after the fifth star had fallen and God's voice went silent. The people in the dream (including myself) rejoiced when the God of heaven stopped speaking because no human could endure the sound of His Voice. In the dream, children were actually rejoicing and bringing out balloons to celebrate for not having to endure the sound of His voice.

I thought a lot about this dream and wondered how mankind preferred not to hear the voice of God by not obeying His commandments. I was deeply saddened to know that men are not fearing God just because we cannot see Him or hear Him audibly.

I was also reminded of the scripture in Revelation 9 the 1st part of verse 1, which talks about the 5th Angel sounding his trumpet – see the following dream about Revelation 9.

I) REVELATION 9 DREAM

In this terrifying dream, I saw a shooting star fall from heaven and when it hit the earth, the ground broke up in pieces and big chunks of earth were floating apart in different directions. Chaos ensued and people fled for their lives. In between the chunks of earth, deep dark chasms became visible and smoke was coming up from the deep abyss. I found myself floating on one of the pieces of earth, holding on for dear life, crying out to God for mercy. In the meantime, smoke and debris were filling up the sky and dark clouds were covering the sky, looking very ominous,

I woke up terrified and immediately, the chapter of Revelation 9 came to my mind. I took the Bible to check scripture and this is what is written there. Verse 1 "Then the 5th *Angel sounded and I saw a star falling from heaven to the earth. To him was given the key to the bottomless pit (verse 2) And he opened the bottomless pit like the smoke of a great furnace, so the sun and the air were darkened because of the smoke of the pit."(NKJV)*

I noted that there is a correlation between this dream and the previous one, where five stars had fallen and God spoke after every star has fallen to the earth.

Also another related scripture written is Isaiah 24 verse 19 -20. *"The earth is violently broken, the earth is split open. The earth is shaken exceedingly. The earth shall reel to and fro like a drunkard and shall totter like a hut. It's transgression shall be heavy upon it and it will fall and not rise again."(NKJV)*

J) Fire falling from the sky

I dreamed that the sky was covered with very dark and ominous clouds and thunder and lightning sounded and flashed and fire fell down from the sky. A voice was speaking from the heavens, telling the story of Jesus from His birth to His resurrection. In the dream, I knew that it was the day of judgement and I started running to go and warn others. I ran as fast as I possibly could to my sister to tell her what was happening. As I was running, a thought came into my mind that as fast as I was running then, so fast we have to go and tell people about the coming of Jesus.

When I got to my sister's house, I was sobbing bitterly as I was relating the story to her. I woke up with a feeling of despair and deep pain for all of humanity.

K) The hour has come (9/11)

It was on the 9th of September 2001 that I had this dream and two days later, when 9/11 happened, I realised that God had given us a prophetic warning. In the dream, I saw one star move, then a second star, then a 3rd star, and soon all the stars in the sky were in motion. I woke up from this dream very amazed and wondered what it could mean. I fell asleep again and the dream continued. This time, everything had disappeared and the whole universe was filled with a very bright white light that we could not imagine in the natural. Then Jesus spoke into my spirit and said, *"FATHER, THE HOUR HAS COME, GLORIFY YOUR SON SO THAT YOUR SON MAY GLORIFY YOU"* (NKJV). This scripture is found in John 17 verse 1 Jesus prayer for the disciples and all His followers.

I woke up even more amazed than the first time.

For the 3rd time, I fell asleep and this time, as the dream still continued, I was telling the dream to everyone I came in contact with because I was filled with such awe about what God had shown me, especially Jesus words in John 17 verse 1. It was spoken to me so clearly.

This dream made me understand that we are already living in the last hour. We do not know how long an hour is in God's time frame, but we have to continue living as if the Lord could return on any day.

Matthew 24 verse 29 "The stars will fall from heaven and the powers of heaven will be shaken" (NKJV)

L) STARS IN MOTION

I had different dreams in which I had seen the stars in motion. In Some of my dreams, I even saw the planets looking big and awesome, visible to the naked eye. In one particular dream, I saw a bright star in the

North and one in the West. Out of these stars appeared other stars and they just kept coming, like the stars were birthing smaller stars.

The Bible does predict that God will shake the heavens and the earth. See the scripture below:

Haggai 2 verse 6-7 "For thus says the Lord of Hosts "Once more (in a little while) I will shake the heavens and the earth, the sea and dry land. And they shall come to the Desire of all nations and I will fill this temple with the Glory " says the Lord of Hosts." (NKJV)

It has been revealed to me by the Holy Spirit that in this verse "The Desire of all nations" is referring to Jesus to Whom every knee will bow.

M) THE MOON PLUMMETING

The moon moved out of its orbit and plummeted down towards the Earth. I panicked since I was aware of the gravity of the moon and the tidal effects that it has on the earth. Also knew (in the dream) that it could have catastrophic consequences for the earth.

N) PLANETS BEING VISIBLE

I called my siblings with great excitement to come and see the planets being visible in the sky with the naked eye. I said to them that this was a sign of the rapture because the Bible says that there will be signs in the sky before the coming of the Lord.

O) TWO MOONS

I dreamed of two moons in the sky in different dreams. Many people have had dreams about two moons in the sky.

P) RED MOON RISING

A bright, big red moon was rising in the east and at the same time, I noticed a sickle moon in the sky. This is another dream about two moons, which might also just relate to an end-time scenario.

Q) MESSAGE TO THE CHURCH

I had a dream where a woman was standing at the pulpit. She was dressed like a prostitute, her hair and make-up showed that she was a prostitute. The sad thing was that she was allowed to preach in the church to the congregation, but I did not want to hear the message, so I walked out of the building. I perceived it to be the "adulterated" church that the Bible talks about – people teaching and following strange doctrines.

After this dream, I experienced that it was breathed into my nostrils and that I was to give a message to the church about the practises and doctrines that were being allowed into the church at this hour.

The scripture that was given to me at this time was Ezekiel 3 verse 10 *"Son of man receive into your heart all My Words that I speak to you and hear with your ears."(NKJV)*

This message serves as a warning to the church to turn back to God, to teach the truth of God's Word to His people and not be defiled with strange doctrines. Jesus told His disciples to feed His sheep and not let the flock be indoctrinated by teachings other than the God's Word.

Let this also be a word of warning to false teachers who deliberately sell out the church members to the God of this world. These wolves in sheep's clothing couldn't care less about the salvation of souls, winning people to Christ to inherit eternal life. God is warning us to turn from their errors and fear Him, who can destroy both body and soul in hell. Why would you sell your eternal soul for the things of the world that are fleeting while you have an eternal soul that could never die but can inherit eternal life in Christ. God gave all humans a free choice. I recently learned of a famous person who would not allow any man to date his daughter unless the person is a billionaire. I was so sad for the girl because to her own father, her worldly happiness is most important. A parent cannot give their child a greater gift than the gift of Christ, Who gives eternal life to those who believe and accept His gift of salvation.

To the well-meaning people who truthfully want to serve God, get familiar with God's Word and pray for discernment. Remember Jesus warning in Matthew 24 verse 4 to 5 *"Take heed that no one deceives you. For many will come in My Name saying "I am the Christ" and will deceive many." (NKJV) T*he deception will be so great that Jesus warns us further in verse *22 "And unless those days will be shortened, no flesh will be saved, but for the elect's sake those days will be shorte*ned. (NKJV)

Even now, well-meaning people follow any leader who declares himself a messenger of God. Now, there is a new person declaring himself to be the successor of Christ and claiming to be the only legitimate pope, without naming anyone specifically. The sad thing is that he already has followers who pledged allegiance to him. Jesus needs no successor. He is the Alpha and Omega, the First and the last, the beginning and the end. Any person (prophet) who came after Christ, bringing another message in addition to the only true Gospel, should be scrutinized in the light of scripture.

Jesus said in John 5 verses 43 to 48 *"I have come in My Father's Name and you did not receive me. If another comes in his own name him you will receive. How can you believe who receive honour from one another and do not seek honour that comes from the only God. Do not think that I shall accuse you to the Father, there is one who accuses you - Moses in whom you trust. For if you believe Moses you would believe Me for he wrote about Me. But if you do not believe his writings how will you believe My words. (NKJV)*

R) GOD IS OUR REFUGE AND STRENGTH

Explosions ripped through the sky, followed by waves of light. Mountains and forests, cities and monstrous tidal waves all appeared at once before my eyes. The mountains started to crumble, the waves of the ocean roared and avalanches headed towards us. Amid all this chaos, the face of the Anti-Christ appeared, making everything appear more dark and sinister. There was nowhere to escape. My sister and I knew that there was no point in trying to get to safety but that we had to take refuge in Him - under the shadows of His wings.

Psalm 46 verse 1 to 3 reads "God is our refuge and strength. A very present help in trouble. Therefore we will not fear even though the earth be removed, And though the mountains be carried into the midst of the sea; though the waters roar and be troubled. Though the mountains shake with it's swelling". (NKJV)

S) THE BEREAN CALL

A word of knowledge came into my spirit, a word that I had never thought of before, but the Holy Spirit was at work again and told me this; "THE BEREAN CALL". I had not planned to write about it, it never crossed my mind, but clearly, the Holy Spirit had spoken. And I knew right away that God wanted me to heed His voice, so wanting to be obedient, I decided to do some homework. I discovered in the book of Acts that during the time of evangelism by the apostles, Paul had taught in a Jewish Synagogue in Berea to the Bereans who were eager to learn more about the Gospel and about Jesus Christ. However, they did not just accept Paul's words, but they examined the Old Testament scriptures to see if what Paul was teaching them was the truth. They were very wise in their decision to read the scriptures and found that what Paul was teaching was verified in the Old Testament scriptures. For this act, Paul referred to them as "noble". They did what God would want all of His people to do today - to study scripture and ask for discernment - not just accept what you are taught by other "prophets", especially not in today's world full of deceit and strange teachings. (NKKJV)

CHAPTER 11
MY REVELATION OF JESUS

A) VISIONS OF JESUS

In a few visions, I saw the face of Jesus in His human form and I was startled by His appearance. I "saw" His profile, as well as Him directly looking at me. These were different visions but it was the same face that I had seen. In another vision, I saw Him hanging on the cross in agony and this vision gave me a shock, seeing the pain and agony on His face.

In yet a different vision, He was leaning over a cliff, extending His arm to me to pull me up out of danger and while leaning over to save me I "saw" a very big teardrop falling from His face. I don't know what I was doing over the cliff. It was probably one of those "many situations" where His children (me in this case) strayed from His ways.

In all the visions that I had, His face always appeared the same to me. I do not claim to know that I know what He looks like, as no one can make that claim. Maybe the visions were given to me to experience Him in a way I could perceive Him – in a way that I could relate to Him. But in His divinity as the King of Heaven, we will all have to wait for the fullness of time to see Him as He is. After all, we are commanded not to make an image of God for ourselves or anything for that matter and bow down to it and worship it as a god. Our God is in heaven and lives within the hearts of believers through His Spirit. I personally do not accept any image of Jesus in my home, as we do not know what He looks like and if we believe the image to be Him, we might be tempted to worship before it.

B) THE HAND OF THE LORD

In this dream, the hand of the Lord pointed out a verse in scripture to me that talks about walking by faith throughout my spiritual journey with Him on the earth. It is a very difficult thing to follow Jesus going through all kinds of trials, especially when you have to avoid worldly pleasures, run the race with endurance and keep your eyes focused on the things of God. It is so tempting when things go very wrong to give up on your hardship and embrace the temptations of the world.

Psalm 119 verse 173 "Let Your Hand become my help, for I have chosen Your precepts" (NKJV)

C) GOD'S CALLING A PERMANENT EXPERIENCE

The words "be sure to make God's calling of you a permanent experience" – this word kept coming into my mind and I later found the scripture in *2 Peter 1 verse 10 – 11 "Therefore brethren be even more diligent to make your call and election sure, for if you do these things, you will never stumble, for so an entrance will be supplied to you abundantly into the everlasting Kingdom of our Lord and Savior, Jesus Christ.* (NKJV)

This was the Holy Spirit giving me words of knowledge again and making me understand that I need to walk in obedience to Him. At the time, I did not work on the calling as hard as I do now because I did not understand His plans for me yet. God has been very patient with me for all these years and I regret wasting so many years of my life.

D) JESUS PUNISHES MY ENEMIES

I had a dream where my enemies (some evil men) were chasing me in the dark and I was trying to get away from them as they were trying to catch up with me. Jesus saw that I was being pursued by evil men and when I looked back, I saw that He was raining down on them some punishment in the form of thunder and lightning. I woke up very relieved that my "Miracle" had come to my rescue once again.

E) HEAVENLY AND EARTHLY FATHERS

This dream was a little vague, but I remember thinking of both my heavenly and earthly fathers. I also saw a vision of Jesus dying on the cross and felt extremely sad about it. I addressed Him as "Father,"

I could remember nothing else about the dream, but it was obvious to me that I could approach Him as my Father.

1 John 3 verses 1 - 2 says," *Behold what manner of love the Father has bestowed on us that we could be called children of God. Therefore, the world does not know us because it did not know Him. Beloved now we are children of God but it had not been revealed what we shall be, but we know that when He is revealed, we shall be like Him for we shall see Him as He is."* (NKJV)

F) LOVE SONG FOR THE LORD

I was playing the most beautiful piece of classical music for Jesus, a worship song on the piano. I did not play the song – all I had to do was to let the Holy Spirit direct my fingers and they just glided over the piano keys and the most beautiful sounds came forth. I was so sure that I would remember the tune, but unfortunately, it did not turn out that way. Perhaps I thought that kind of music was only allowed in heaven.

In another dream, I was asleep on my bed when my spirit was awakened by some heavenly music. My spirit was aware that my body was asleep. Then, in my spirit, I heard the most beautiful heavenly love and worship song for the Lord. My spirit was singing along and everything, the tune, the melody and the lyrics of the song were crystal clear to me. I was convinced that I would remember the melody and the words and even contemplating to compose the song. After I had awakened, I remembered nothing of the melody or the lyrics.

The Bible says that we must give thanks to God and give praises to Him through Psalms and melody and singing in our hearts.

Psalm 50 verse 23 says, "Whoever offers praise Me glorifies Me,"

G) HOLY FEAR OF GOD

I experienced the Holy fear of God in this dream but did not dream of anything specific. Just encountered the presence of the Lord. (Revelation 15 verse 4) "Who shall not fear *Thee O Lord. And glorify Your Name. For You alone are Holy. For all nations shall come and worship before you."(NKJV)*

In another dream, God had spoken to me again in a fearsome voice, giving me personal instructions and a word of knowledge,

Prov 2v1-5 "My son if you receive my word and treasure my commandments within you, then you will incline your ear to wisdom and apply your heart to understanding. Yes If you cry out for discernment and lift up your voice for understanding. If you seek her as silver and search for her as hidden treasures. Then you will understand the fear of the Lord." (NKJV)

Proverbs 15 verse 33 "The fear of the Lord is the instruction of wisdom." (NKJV)

I cannot say much about the fear of the Lord other than that which is written in scripture. But what I can say is the fear of Him that I had experienced in some of my dreams and encounters is not something that could be taken lightly. Scripture also warns us th*at "It is a fearful thing to fall into the Hands of the Living God." Hebrews 10 verse 31. (NKJV)*

H) THE BLESSINGS OF ABRAHAM

In this dream, God reminded me of the promises that He had given me before (in a previous dream) that as He had promised Abraham to bless him with His descendants as numerous as the stars of heaven, so will He bless me. The promise of a blessing upon me remained a mystery to me until the Holy Spirit revealed the truth of this promise to me – that it is none other than Christ Himself, as I discovered in the following verse:

Galatians 1 verse 13 "Christ has redeemed us from the curse of the Law, having become u curse for us (for it is written "Cursed is everyone who hangs on a tree") Verse 14 That the <u>blessings of Abraham</u> may come upon the Gentiles in Christ Jesus, that we might receive the promise of the Spirit through faith."(NKJV)

In Genesis 15 verse 5 God said to Abraham, "Look now toward the heavens and count the stars if you are able to number them. And He said to him: so shall your descendants be." (Meaning the spiritual descendants of Abraham in Christ).

In this promise, God did talk about the natural descendants of Abraham only but also spoke about all the spiritual descendants as written in Genesis 18 verse 18 God had made the promise that "All the nations of the world will be blessed in Him."

Let us keep this precious promise in our hearts and strive to follow Christ at all costs, even if we do not see our rewards here on earth. God's Word is true. His promises are "Yes and "Amen." He promises us that no one can know what He has in store for us in heaven.

I) RECOGNIZING HIS DIVINITY

The recognition of Jesus's Divinity had become more evident to me over the years of Jesus revealing Himself to me through the dreams and visions as well as the revelation I have received through His Word.

Ephesians 1 verse 17 says, "that the God of our Lord Jesus Christ, the Father of Glory, may give you the spirit of wisdom and revelation in the knowledge of Him."

When Jesus had asked the disciples in Mark 8 verse 27-29 *"Who do you say I AM"* They answered Him *"You are the Son of the Living God"* to which He replied that flesh and blood did not reveal it to them, but the Father in heaven". Refer to the verse in 1 Corinthians 12 verse 3 where scripture says *that no-one can say that Jesus is Lord except by the Holy Spirit.* Here is where I urge the reader to seek Him with all their heart and ask Jesus to reveal himself to you and He will. You cannot believe that Jesus is Lord if you haven't received His Spirit within you. No one can enter the Kingdom of God if you haven't received the new birth by the Spirit of the Living God. See John chapter 3 where Nicodemus questioned Jesus as to how a man could be born again.

Once the Holy Spirit has revealed the divinity of Christ to you, then you will not doubt that He is who He says He is. Receiving and believing the Gospel is a spiritual matter and you cannot rely on your natural mind to teach you the truth about Jesus. Apostle Paul reminds us in *1 Corinthians 2 verse 14, "But the natural mind does not receive the things of the Spirit of God for they are foolishness to him, nor can he know them for they are spiritually discerned." (NKJV)*

I see Jesus throughout the Old Testament right into the New. He had told us repeatedly in the Old Testament that He is God, the Savior of mankind. There cannot be another Savior but God Himself. I just wonder why, for some it is so difficult to understand that the God who created the universe could come to the earth in the flesh and still remain the Omniscient Creator. Nothing is impossible with God. We cannot comprehend His power and His wisdom.

In Job 26 we read about the Power of God. This whole chapter is such a beautiful passage, but I am quoting from verses 12-14 *"He stirs up the sea with His power and by His understanding, He breaks up the storm. By His Spirit, He adorned the heavens. His Hand pierced the fleeing serpent. Indeed, these are the mere edges of His ways and how small a whisper we hear of Him. But the thunder of His Power, Who can understand?" (NKJV)*

I have described in detail in different dreams and visions how the Lord has revealed Himself to me, that He is the God of the Bible. Refer to chapter 5 about Jesus showing me in my dreams that He represents all the attributes of the Godhead mentioned in the Bible. He came to me as the "Word" from heaven, the bread of life, the bright Morning star and light of the world, the Ancient of days, the One born in the flesh to be King and many others. In a few dreams, He even tested me to see if I would recognize Him as Lord, and by His Grace, I did have the discernment to "see" Him with my spiritual eyes.

J) MY PRAISES TO THE KING OF GLORY

I cannot help but stand in awe of who God is. All the works that He has done with His right Hand. This brings me to share with you that I understand Jesus to be the right hand of God, the arm of the Lord. I know many of you understand this already, but I have come to not only understand this fact by the teaching of His Word but also through His own revelations to me. Habakkuk

3 verse to 4. *"His Glory covered the heavens and the earth was full of His praise. His brightness was like the light. He had rays from flashing from His Hand and there His power was hidden. (NKJV)*

Since God is a Trinity, yet One God only, who manifests Himself to us through His Son, we can only come to faith through the Son. Many people cannot understand the Triune God, but to those whom He reveals Himself to, it is not too hard to understand it by faith. However, we cannot fully comprehend it because of our limited human understanding of God. Of course, we cannot fully grasp who He is in all of His power, but we understand it in our spirits because He has revealed Himself to us. I have received my own revelations through His Glorious Spirit and that is why I can share my heart with you.

I stand in awe of the God of all creation, who came into the world as a humble man to pay the price for our eternal souls, yet mankind has rejected him, but to those who have accepted Him," *He gave the right to become the children of God."*

I stand in awe of everything in nature that God has created, the mighty ocean, with many undiscovered forms of life and treasures unknown. I am amazed at the majestic mountains *(Before the mountains were brought forth. Or ever You had formed the earth and the world, from everlasting to everlasting, You are God. (Psalm 90 verse 2) (NJKV)*

The beauty of nature declares His wisdom and His power. The birds of the air and the flowers of the field all sing of the praises of His Majesty. He made the stars for His Glory and scripture says that He knows them all by Name.

The beasts of the field, all living things in the ocean, rivers and lakes. They all testify of the greatness and the power of the Highest. All animals – I often wondered how animals know how to behave according to their kind. God has put everything they need for survival in their DNA. Even they know how to love. The love and loyalty I have received from my own pets over the years tell me of the Love of God for all of His creation. It is no coincidence that God has blessed us with everything we need in life without us being appreciative and thankful, taking everything things for granted.

Revelation 11 verse 17 "We give thanks to You O Lord God Almighty. The One Who is and Who was and Who is to come. Because You have taken Your great power and reigned."(NKJV)

CHAPTER 12
THE JESUS MIRACLE

A) THE WORD OF THE LORD:

I understand Jesus to be the One who had appeared to the prophets throughout the Old Testament scriptures as the "The Word of the Lord." In the New Testament, we read in John Chapter 1 verse 1, "In the beginning was the Word and the Word was with God and the Word was God." From this verse, I understand it to be the same Word that had appeared to the prophets. "He was in the beginning with God. All things were made by Him and without Him, nothing was made that was made."

Also, in Psalm 33 verse 6 we read, *"By the Word of the Lord the heavens were made and all their hosts by the breath of His mouth"*. Jesus is the Word by whom everything was made, "by Him through Him and for him".

In Revelation 19 verse 13 the scriptures tell us that "He was clothed with a robe dipped in blood and His Name is called "The Word of God." (NKJV)

We know that this word is speaking about the sacrificial death that Jesus died on the cross for the sins of the world.

In the Old Testament, God had appeared many times to the prophets as "THE WORD OF THE LORD."

B) THE ANGEL OF THE LORD

In many passages of the Old Testament, Jesus is referred to as the Angel of the Lord or the Word of the Lord. When reading through the book of Revelation, the Lord makes it clear to us in His Word that Jesus is the eternal God who had been speaking to us through His Living Word and through the prophets. In Revelation 22 verse 16 God says, "I, Jesus, have sent My Angel (This is God Himself speaking, referring to Himself as Jesus) to testify these things in the churches.

In Judges 13, The Angel of the Lord appeared to Minoah and his wife. The Angel conveyed a message to Minoah's wife that although she was barren and bore no children, she would conceive and bear a son. In verse 6 we read that the woman told her husband that, "I saw a Man of God Whose countenance was like the *countenance of the Angel of God, very awesome, but I did not ask Him where He was from and He did not tell me His Name."* (NKJV)

Further on in this chapter, Minoah prayed to God to send the Man of God again so he could put his own questions to Him. When He asked the Angel of the Lord if he could stay with them so they could prepare a meal for Him, the Angel of the Lord answered and said to him that He could not eat their food, even if He stayed with them, but if he offered a burnt offering", He must offer it to the Lord "For Minoah did not know that HE WAS THE ANGEL OF THE LORD."

When Minoah did the burnt offering to the Lord, a wonderful thing happened: the angel of the Lord ascended in the flames towards heaven. When the Angel of the Lord appeared to them no more, they fell on their faces to the ground and Minoah said to his wife. "We shall surely die for we have seen God."

(see Judges 13 verse 19-22)

C) HIS NAME IS WONDERFUL

I have always been amazed why God refers to His own Name as a Name of Wonder. His Name is all-encompassing and He cannot just have a Name that has one meaning. When Moses had asked Him his

Name, His answer was 'I am". God knows that we could not comprehend His divine nature from the Name that He revealed to Moses.

In Judges 13 verses 17 and 18, we read, "And Minoah said to the Angel "What is Your Name that when Your words came to pass we may honor You." And the Angel of the Lord said to him, "Why do you ask My name, seeing it is a <u>Name of</u> <u>wonder?"</u>

D) THE SON OF GOD, THE SON OF MAN

Jesus was promised as the Savior to the whole world, even throughout the Old Testament scriptures. Who else but God Himself can walk on water, raised the dead, forgive sins, heal the sick, set the captives free, rise from the dead, ascended to heaven, proclaimed Himself One with God and demonstrated His love towards us, that while we were sinners, Christ died for us.

He claimed that He and the Father are One and that whoever has seen Him has seen the Father when He was questioned by His disciples. Also, Jesus said to His disciples that whoever is of God hears God's voice, but those who do not listen to His voice is not of God.

Psalm 8 verses 3-5 "When I consider the heavens, the works of your fingers, the moon and the stars which You have ordained. What is man that you are mindful of him. _The Son of man_ that you visit him. You have made him a little lower than the angels but have crowned him with glory and honour."(NKJV)

In Hebrews 2 we learn that the "Son of man" spoken of in Psalm 8 verse 5 speaks about God who became a man (Jesus) to be made a little lower than the Angels in order to be crowned with Glory and Honor after conquering death and received up in (Glory) into heaven.

Jesus says in John 14 verse 7 _"If you had known Me you would have known the Father also and from now on you know Him and have seen Him."(NKJV)_

In Psalm 22 He says, "But You are He who took Me out of My mother's womb. You made Me trust while on My mother's breasts. I was cast upon You from birth. From My mother's womb You have been My God."(NKJV)

This passage is also clear to me that God had made a statement that He would come to us in the flesh, however, many things about Messiah are hidden in scripture. To me the Lord Jesus had been there all along but some of us did not see Him. He has to reveal this to you if you are hungry enough for Him and if you seek Him with all your heart. Draw near to Him and He will draw near to you. He is the "hidden treasure" and the "pearl of great price" that we need to search for.

He told His disciples that if they did not believe that He is from God, they should believe Him because of the works He does.

1 Timothy 1 verse 16 "And without controversy, great is the mystery of godliness. "God was manifested in the flesh, justified in the Spirit, Seen by Angels, preached among the Gentiles, believed on in the world, received up in Glory." (NKJV)

In Philippians 2 we read that *Christ who was in the form of God did not consider diminishing God by making Himself equal with God, but He made Himself of no reputation, coming in the likeness of man. He humbled Himself and became obedient to the point of death.*

Let's consider Isaiah 53 verse 2-3 *"For He shall grow up before Him as a tender plant and as a root out of dry ground. He had no form or comeliness and when we see Him, there is no beauty that we should desire Him. He is despised and rejected by men. A man of sorrows and acquainted with grief and we hid as it were our faces from Him. He was despised and we did not esteem Him."(NKJV)*

Many people deny that God could have become a Man, but He has made mention of this in the scriptures Himself; that this would indeed be fulfilled.

This child that has been promised to Israel first and then to the whole world had already been born, and many had not recognized Him when He came when the words of the prophets came to pass 2000 years ago.

E) THE SERVANT OF THE LORD

Jesus had referred to Himself in the Gospels as a "Servant". He came to serve and draw many to Himself. To demonstrate His Servitude, He even washed the feet of His disciples.

In Isaiah 49 verse 5 He says that the Lord formed Him in the womb to be His Servant to bring Jacob back to Him so that Israel is gathered to Him. ("For I shall be glorious in the eyes of the Lord"}

Here are more scriptures relating to the Servanthood of Messiah

Isaiah 42 verse 1 "Behold My Servant whom I uphold. My elect One in whom my soul delights. I have put My Spirit upon Him. He will bring forth justice to the Gentiles."(NKJV)

Jeremiah 11 verse 19 "But I was like a docile lamb brought to the slaughter and I did not know that they devised schemes against Me, saying "Let us destroy the tree with its fruit and let us cut him off from the land of the living that His name be remembered no more,"(NKJV)

Isaiah 43 verse 10 "You are My witnesses says the Lord My Servant whom I have chosen that you may know and believe Me and understand that I AM HE. Before Me there was no God formed nor shall there be after Me."(NKJV)

I would also recommend that you read and study Psalm 22 which is a Psalm about the Messiah. Everything in this passage speaks about the events that unfolded at the cross with the crucifixion of Jesus,

In Isaiah 49 verse 5-8 God plainly declares that He would come as a servant, in the flesh, to bring salvation not only to the Jews but also to the Gentiles.

F) THE GOD OF ISRAEL

God has revealed to us through scripture that it had been His plan and His desire since the fall of man to reconcile all of humanity to Him. The plan has always been there and He made it known to His people Israel, through the prophets. All humans were created in God's image and for His glory, and He had chosen His people, Israel through which salvation would come to the world – "to the Jews first and also to the Gentiles."

Romans 1 verse 16 "For I am not ashamed of the Gospel of Christ for it is the power of God to Salvation, for the JEWS FIRST AND ALSO FOR THE GREEK."

Through the nation of Israel, Messiah was born so that God could reconcile Jew and gentile to Himself as "One new man" – the spirit man who inherits eternal life through Jesus Christ.

Ephesians 2 verse 14 to 15 "For He Himself is our Peace who has made both one and has broken down the middle wall of separation, having abolished in His flesh, the enmity, that is, the Law of commandments contained in ordinances so as to create in Himself ONE NEW MAN from the two thus making peace."(NKJV)

We, the Gentiles serve the true and living God of Israel who gave Himself (in the flesh) as a Ransom to many – to all those who would believe, to the Jew first and also to the Gentiles. We are truly blessed that Israel's God has been mindful of the "Nations" to bring them to salvation together with His people so that we had become one new man in Messiah. That is why true Christians love the Jewish people because their God is our God. True believers will always stand with Israel - they are our brothers and sisters in Messiah.

There are many scriptures in the Old Testament that speak about the God of Israel who would bring the nations into His inheritance.

In Psalm 2 verses 7 - 8 the Word reads, "I will declare the decree. "The Lord has said to Me "You are My Son today

I have begotten You. Ask of Me and I will give You the nations for Your inheritance and the ends of the earth for Your possession." (NKJV)

God speaks about Himself as "The Son" and throughout the scriptures, He sometimes speaks about Himself in plural and here is where the Holy Spirit has given me wisdom and understanding. Thereby, God is referred to as "The Son of God" as well as the "Son of man."

Below are some scripture verses to be considered and studied. Ask God for wisdom and guidance to open your heart to understanding His Word.

Psalm 22 verse 27 "All the ends of the world shall remember and turn to the Lord. And all the families of the nations shall worship before You. For the Kingdom is the Lord's and He rules over the nations. (NKJV)

1 Samuel *22 verse 44 "You have delivered Me from the strivings of My people. You have kept me as the head of the nations. A people I have not known shall serve me. The foreigner submits to Me. As soon as they hear they obey Me."(NKJV)*

Isaiah 44 verse 6 "Thus says the Lord, the King of Israel and His Redeemer the Lord of hosts. I am the first and I am the last. Besides Me there is no God." (NKJV)

Jesus says in Revelation 1 verses 17 – 18 "Do not be afraid. I Am the First and the Last. I Am He who lives and was dead. And behold I Am alive forevermore. Amen." (NKJV)

Isaiah 43 verse 13 "Indeed before the day was, I AM HE. And there is no-one who can deliver out of My hand. I work and who will reverse it."(NKJV)

Isaiah 47 verse 4 "As for our Redeemer, the Lord of hosts is His Name. The Holy One of Israel." (NKJV)

G) PROMISES TO THE NATIONS

The God of Israel has made many promises to the nations (gentiles) that He would save everyone - to the ends of the earth, who would believe in His Name and in His promises. He is a God of love and "He is not willing that anyone should perish, but that everyone should come to Him in faith and receive eternal life through the God of Salvation – Yeshua (Which means salvation).

Scriptures to study for your own understanding of Him:

Isaiah 45 verses 22-23 "Look to me all ye ends of the earth. For I am God and there is no other. I have sworn by Myself, the Word has gone out of my mouth in righteousness, that to Me every knee shall bow and every tongue shall take an oath."(NKJV)

Isaiah 47 verse 4 "As for our Redeemer, the Lord of hosts is His Name. The Holy One of Israel."

Isaiah 49 verse 5-7 "And now the Lord says who formed Me from the womb to be His servant to bring Jacob back to Him so that Israel is gathered to Him (For I shall be glorious in the eyes of the Lord. My God shall be my strength.) Indeed, He says, it is too small a thing that You should be My servant to raise up the tribes of Jacob and to restore the preserved ones of Israel. <u>I will also give You as a light to the Gentiles, that You should be MY salvation to the ends of the earth.</u>"(NKJV)

Isaiah 51 verses 4 to 5 "Listen to Me MY people and give ear to Me O My nation. For law will proceed from Me. And I will make My justice rest as a light of the peoples. My righteousness is near My salvation has gone forth and My arm will judge the peoples. The coastlands will wait upon Me and on My arm they will trust. (NKJV)

Isaiah 60 verse 3 "The Gentiles shall come to your light and kings to the glory of your rising."(NKJV)

Isaiah 60 verse 5 "Then you shall see and become radiant and your heart shall swell with joy because the abundance of the sea shall be turned to you. The wealth of the Gentiles shall come to you." (NKJV)

Here, I understand that "the wealth of the Gentiles" indicates the ones who came to the Jewish Messiah by faith in Jesus Christ and by accepting the free gift of salvation.

Isaiah 45 verses 6-7 "I the Lord have called You in righteousness and will hold Your hand. I will keep You and give You as a covenant to the people, as a light to the Gentiles to open blind eyes and to bring out prisoners from the prison. Those who sit in darkness from the prison house."(NKJV)

Isaiah 45 verses 22-23 "Look to me all ye ends of the earth. For I am God and there is no other. I have sworn by Myself, the Word has gone out of my mouth in righteousness, that to Me every knee shall bow and every tongue shall take an oath." (NKJV)

H) THE HIDDEN ONE

In the Old Testament, God has promised Israel to give them a Servant like Moses and that they should listen to Him. The prophets were all aware of the promise of Messiah that He would be born in Bethlehem and that He would be a light to the nations. In all of history, Jesus has been the only one who fulfilled the prophecy. There were many prophecies predicting the coming of the Messiah. In some of the passages in Isaiah, the Lord says that He Himself will be the Savior of the World and that He will be the One who speaks on that day. Jesus came and spoke to the people and claimed that He is One with God.

Here are some scripture verses that testify about this.

Isaiah 45 verse 15 "Truly You are God who hides Yourself, O God of Israel the Savior."(NKJV)

Isaiah 49 verses 1-2" Listen O coastlands to Me and take heed O people from afar. The Lord has called Me from the womb. From the matrix of My mother, He has made mention of My Name. And He has made my mouth like a sharp sword. In the shadow of His hand, He has hidden Me and made Me a polished shaft. In His quiver He has hidden Me."(NKJV)

Paul tells us in Ephesians 2 that "he had been given the grace to preach the unsearchable riches of Christ among the gentiles and to make everyone see the mystery of Christ which has been hidden in God from the beginning of the ages and that God has created all things through Christ". (NKJV)

*Isaiah 48 verses 16-17 "Come near to me and hear this. I have not spoken in secret from the beginning. From the time that it was, I was there. And now the Lord <u>God and His Spirit *have sent Me.</u>" (NKJV)*

In this verse I clearly understand and see the doctrine of the Trinity.

It is very clear from scripture that Jesus is the One who had always been One with God. Christ was Hidden in God from us since before the foundation of the world. It is confirmed by John in chapter 1 that *"He was in the beginning with God. "All things were made by Him and without Him nothing was made that was made."* *(NKJV)*

I) YESHUA OUR SALVATION

Jesus's Name in Hebrew means Salvation. He came as the Savior of the World, not only for Israel but also for the whole world. It is all written in the scriptures. We just need to study our Bibles and ask God to reveal to us the hidden truth in the Bible. The Bible is the Living Word of God. God speaks to us through the Bible. I seriously recommend that you get familiar with scripture and ask the Holy Spirit to teach you so that you will be able to understand His Word. Only by the Spirit can the Word become alive in your heart. You cannot understand the Word of God completely in your natural mind only. Jesus says "It is the Spirit that gives life. The flesh profits nothing. *The words that I speak to you, they are spirit and they are life."* *John 6 verse 63.* (NKJV)J

127

Look at Hebrews 12 verse 4 which says *"For the Word of God is living and powerful, sharper than any double-edged sword, piercing even to the division of soul and spirit and of joints and marrow and is a discerner of the thoughts and intents of the hearts of men."*

The Lord made known to Israel that He had not spoken in secret that He had always been there from the beginning, that no one can deliver out of His Hand. The God of Israel says in Isaiah 43 verse 13 that "I Am He". So, who is He referring to that will do the work that no one can deliver out of His Hand? Jesus is the only One in history who has finished the work at the cross. He said that there was no one to help Him and that "HIS OWN ARM" had brought Him Salvation and that His own righteousness had sustained Him. This the holy Spirit has revealed to us that God Himself has brought salvation to His people and to the whole world. The scripture says that God has opened His ear to hear those who had scriptural knowledge and has given Him the tongue of the educated so that He should know how to speak a word in season when He would come to dwell with His people.

God foretold that His Servant would be rejected by many, despised by man and abhorred by nations. (refer to Isaiah 53). Jesus is still being rejected by many today and some people find it offensive that He is seen by His followers as the true One God, who came in the flesh. I understand that some people cannot wrap their minds around that, but once you have received the Holy Spirit, you will know and understand everything that God reveals to you.

Below are some scripture verses for your guidance and understanding.

Isaiah 49 verse 26c "All flesh shall know that I the Lord am your Savior and your Redeemer the mighty One of Jacob."

Isaiah 43 verse 21 "This people I have formed for Myself, they shall declare My praise."

J) OUR GREAT HIGH PRIEST

In the Old Covenant, the high priest had to offer a blood sacrifice for his own sins and also for the sins of the people. The Law appointed priests with weaknesses to be the mediators for the people, but with the New Covenant the Son Himself is appointed as High Priest for He had been perfected through His sacrifice for His people. The high priests were human beings, weak in the flesh but they were specially selected to enter into the presence of God on behalf of the people.

In the new covenant, Jesus became our Great High Priest and offered His own body as a blood sacrifice for the sins of all people once and for all. Scripture says that there is no remission of sins without the shedding of blood. Therefore, God Himself had to come in human likeness as God had to prepare a body for Him that would ultimately be used as a sin offering for the world.

In Genesis 14 verse 18 Melchizedek the King of Salem appeared to Abraham and brought <u>bread and wine</u>. (Jesus said that His body was the bread of Life and His blood He gave as wine to drink – symbolically speaking.) "He was the Priest of the Most High God". Not much is being said about Him in the Old Testament, but in the book of Hebrews in the New Testament we learn more about this mysterious person. We learn from Hebrews that Melchizedek had no genealogy, no beginning of days nor end of life and that He was made" like the Son of God remaining a priest forever". This to me, speaks about Jesus, although He came as a man, he had always been with the Father, for He says "I and the Father are One." (NKJV)

In Hebrews 4 verse 14, we read, "Seeing then that we have a Great High Priest who has passed through the heavens, Jesus the Son of God, let us hold fast our confession for we do not have a High Priest who cannot sympathize with our weaknesses but be in all points tempted as we are yet without sin." (NKJV)

Scripture also says in Hebrews 5 verse 5 that Christ did not glorify Himself to become High Priest but it was He Who said to Him (Father speaking to the Son), "You are My Son, today I have begotten You". Verse 6 "You are a Priest forever according to the Order of Melchizedek."(NKJV)

The Revelation to me is that Yeshua (Salvation) is Melchizedek who had appeared to Abraham.

CONCLUSION

JESUS – THE MIRACLE

From everything the Lord Jesus had taught me by His Spirit, I confess His Name before men and I declare that I am not ashamed of His Name or of the Gospel of Christ. ("The Gospel is the power of God unto Salvation"} Romans 1 verse 16. The Lord God has dealt with me in wonderful ways that I could never have dreamed of. He had chosen me to make His Words known to me and to reveal to me that Jesus is and has always been the King of Israel – the true God. If you search for Him with all of your heart and all of your soul, He will reveal Himself to you as He had done for me.

Besides all the miracles that Jesus had done while on the earth, He is to me also the Miracle working God of all creation. Think back to all the miracles that He had done for Israel: He led them through the wilderness and provided manna (bread from heaven) and water from the rock. He parted the Red Sea and always took care of His people (even though they went astray and went after false gods) and many other miracles mentioned in the Bible like the miracles He performed for His people of Israel.

The miracle that He creates in the heart of every human being who invites Him into their hearts is beyond understanding in our natural minds. The miracle that He is able to do to give us a new heart and put a new spirit within us is something only the God of creation could do. Only a born-again believer will understand what it is to be "born of the spirit" because God has given us His Spirit.

Jesus told Nicodemus in John chapter 3 verse 7-8 *"Do not marvel that I said to you, you must be born again. The wind blows where it wishes, you hear the sound of it. But cannot tell where it comes from and where it goes. So is everyone who is born of the Spirit."(NKJV)*

Finally, as mentioned before, this work is purely the result of what the Holy Spirit has revealed to me and has done in me. I was just His vessel and I was obedient to what the Lord wanted me to do. God's heart is for all people to come to know Him, and I pray that I will be partly instrumental in this calling – a vessel for honour. But all glory and honour to Jesus (Yeshua) to Whom every knee will bow.

He had spoken to me through my dreams even before I had knowledge of scripture. In the beginning, I had no understanding that God wanted me to know Him and to have a relationship with Him. It was a long, winding road, not a straight path at all and I had fallen down many times. By His Spirit and His Word, I would be encouraged to get up and continue my walk with Him.

I just need to caution every person who wants to know the Savior that it is not an easy road to travel. "Many are the afflictions of the righteous but the Lord delivers him out of them all. (Psalm 34 verse 19" (NKJV)

Also, believers are called saints because they have been sanctified by the blood of the Lamb. A saint is not declared a saint by man – a saint is a believer who has received the Spirit of God and thereby is sanctified by His Spirit by believing in the only God who can save and grant eternal life, Jesus Christ the Holy and Mighty One.

Jesus is my Miracle. He had done wonders for me in the spirit. I became a " new creation in Christ." You can too. Make Jesus your miracle today. Ask Him, the God of salvation, to reveal Himself to you. He will if you ask with a sincere heart and genuine faith.

Considering all that the Holy Spirit has revealed to me about Jesus, I think it's no coincidence that He wanted the book to be titled: "The Jesus Miracle."

AMEN AND AMEN.

Bibliography: All scriptures are taken from the New King James Translation.

SOPHIA R. BAILEY

THANKS AND ACKNOWLEDGMENT

First and foremost, to Abba Father, the Lord Jesus Christ, to whom I owe all my praise and adoration for instructing and guiding me in the revelation of the contents of this book. To the Holy Spirit, my teacher and counsellor for the revelation of scripture and dreams and visions. Without You, this book would not have been possible.

To my husband Dennis, who encouraged me to continue with the book and a few family members, thank you for believing in me.

To my dear lifelong friend Erika Kruger for standing by me through very difficult times. You did what no one else would do. I will always have you in my heart. Thank you for your prayers and the sacrifices you have made for me. I will always love you, my sister.

To Diedie, my lifelong friend and sister in Christ who had always been there for me, like Erika. Thank you also for your prayers and loving support when I was in deep despair.

To my spiritual mentors at Didasko years ago, Pastor Neels and Mrs Hannetjiede Klerk, Pastor Jacob Van Schalwyk and Pastor Christiaan Kruger - thank you for being true shepherds of the sheep. Thank you for your guidance in spiritual matters and your overall concern for the well-being of the students at Didasko during 1999. I have learned much from you. May you remain the light in the world that you always have been.

To Werner and Adel Swart, my former Leaders from the Harvest Evangelism team as well as your precious five sons and daughters, It was an honour to serve with you in the Mission Field and I pray you a great harvest for the Lord.

To all my ex-fellow missionary students at Didasko from 1999. It was an honour to serve with you in the Mission Field and just being fellow servants in Christ.

To Juan Cronje, our partner and website designer from True Pic who believed in my story and helped to get us started with the book, Thank you, Juan. May you be blessed richly.

To our dear friend Grant Kuhn, thank you for your advice on the book. You have been a real friend in need.

Thanks to our loved ones for your moral support during the years in our "little Egypt'". You know who you are and you will not be forgotten.

Lastly, I dedicate this book to my late father and mother, Jan and Francina Koetzee for being the parents you were, as well as all my late siblings. I also dedicate the book to all who are hungry for God and hope you will find your own little golden nuggets in this book for your spiritual growth.

I would also like to extend my sincere gratitude and heartfelt appreciation to the entire team at A.M. for believing in my story and for the remarkable way in which you came alongside me during this sacred assignment. Your willingness to reach out, encourage, and walk with me on this journey was not merely professional support but a divine appointment. I truly believe that the Lord used you as the "door" He had promised to open, one that would lead me toward the fulfillment of His calling over my life. Through your dedication and grace, **The Jesus Miracle** has come to life as a testimony of His faithfulness. May God bless each one of you richly for being His vessels of purpose and compassion.